your
promising

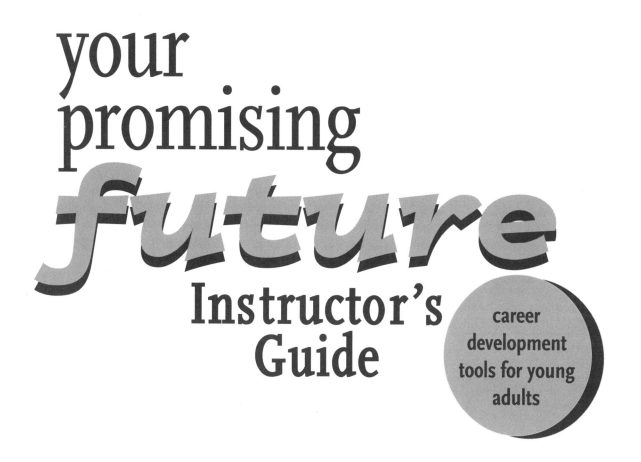

Instructor's Guide

career
development
tools for young
adults

Meta Dunn

Works
America's Career Publisher

Your Promising Future Instructor's Guide

© 2004 by Meta Dunn

Published by JIST Works, an imprint of JIST Publishing, Inc.
8902 Otis Avenue
Indianapolis, IN 46216-1033

Phone: 1-800-648-JIST   Fax: 1-800-JIST-FAX
E-mail: info@jist.com   Web site: www.jist.com

Note to Instructors

This instructor's guide supports *Your Promising Future*, a separate student workbook (1-59357-011-2) based on the highly successful Promising Futures curriculum. A video titled *Exploring Your Career Options* features the author and is available in VHS and DVD formats. Other videos and assessments on job search topics are also available. Call 1-800-648-JIST for details.

Visit our Web site at www.jist.com for information on JIST, free job search information, book excerpts, and ordering information on our many products. For free information on 14,000 job titles, visit www.CareerOINK.com.

Quantity discounts are available for JIST books. Please call our sales department at 1-800-648-JIST for a free catalog and more information.

Acquisitions Editor: Randy Haubner
Development Editor: Barb Terry
Cover Designer: Trudy Coler
Interior Designer: Aleata Howard
Proofreader: Jeanne Clark

Reviewers: Sol Flores, La Casa Norte, Chicago, IL; Suzie Huber, Noblesville High School, Noblesville, IN; Florence Jackson, New York Public Schools; Alice Johnson, Broad Ripple High School, Indianapolis, IN; Toni Lawal, Southwest Tennessee Community College, Memphis, TN; Fred McQueen, Greater Cincinnati Urban League, Cincinnati, OH; Rochelle Perry, Project Return; Beverly Robinson, Arlington High School, Indianapolis, IN; Fidal Young, TRIO Program, Chicago, IL.

Printed in the United States of America

09 08 07 06 05 04   9 8 7 6 5 4 3 2 1

ISBN 1-59357-012-0

About This Instructor's Guide

Do your students have a promising future? Have they heard "you can't" all their lives? Do people constantly point out the obstacles that lie ahead of them? Does "promising future" sound like words that apply to people who live someplace else, or have better grades or stronger families than your students?

Let Meta Dunn, the author of the separate *Your Promising Future* student workbook and this instructor's guide, show you how to light the fire in the hearts of students who've begun to believe that a purposeful, rewarding future is only a dream. She knows what it's like to have heard all the reasons why a successful life is impossible and still found the courage, strength, and direction that made it possible to begin creating the life she wanted. She is the mother of two who made it through to her master's degree despite the fact that people were telling her to get a job, to settle for less than what she really wanted.

Through the activities in the *Your Promising Future* workbook, Meta shows your students that the source of a promising future lies within oneself, within the dreams that make us who we are. This instructor's guide shows you how, step by step, to help each student build a fulfilling future. You'll appreciate the guide's clearly defined objectives, detailed presentation plans, helpful notes and tips, suggestions for additional activities based on learning styles, PowerPoint slides, and assessment questions.

Table of Contents

Introduction

T his instructor's guide and the *Your Promising Future* curriculum have been created in order to better prepare youth from low-income communities for their careers. It provides a hands-on, empowering approach to the career search process. The overlying objective of each chapter is to give each student insight into his or her personal value and see himself or herself as an indispensable asset that companies need. This objective is founded on the belief that all people have unique characteristics that enhance their employability, but oftentimes they are not taught to look for these characteristics, especially when they come from low-income communities. This curriculum aims to identify those characteristics and draw them out of each student who participates in this program.

The key to each activity is to start the students thinking about the purpose of each step in the career search process. The students are then empowered by understanding why they take certain actions. Education and career development are fundamental areas that affect all areas of not only our lives, but also society as a whole. Forsaking knowledge in these areas has and will continue to cause detrimental effects in our society, so it is important that these students learn this.

Realistically, many of the students may not quite understand and will complete the steps just because they are supposed to, but it is necessary to encourage a higher level of processing so that in the future they will connect some of the things they learned in the program. Don't be discouraged if the results are not what you expect. In the long run, the students' lives will be impacted.

In order to effectively deliver the curriculum, it may be best for you, the instructor, to reflect on your own career path and how you made the decision to do the work you are doing, and then share some of your personal stories with the students. It is important for the students to see this path and understand that there is nothing right or wrong about the path one chooses to a career, provided he or she is working toward a goal. Reflecting on your own career path and then being able to articulate it will help students to grow and see that all people go through a discovery and learning process to gain skills and find a job that (hopefully) suits them.

Now let's flip the script a little bit. Your Promising Future is not your run-of-the-mill career development curriculum, and I am not your typical teacher. As a single teen mom with two different "babies-daddies" (of different racial/ethnic backgrounds) putting myself through college and then graduate school, I faced many of the same obstacles many of the students face. As I searched for a way to make it, I taught teens throughout Chicago who faced situations similar to my own. Day in and day out, as I fought my own battles and tried to find some book, program, or class that spoke to my situation, I also struggled to find material that I could use to teach the kids I worked with. Nothing seemed right, so I decided to create my own book.

I wrote *Your Promising Future* to provide a hands-on tool to show youth that, no matter what they may face, they can succeed if they follow their heart. I know because I followed my heart to get to where I am today: in my twenties, two children, a master's degree, with a published book, doing what I love to do—and I stayed on a straight path to do it!

1

As I said, though, I am not your typical teacher. In fact, I have taught in classrooms for more than five years, but I have no formal teaching degree. My Bachelor's is in Social Work and my Master's is in Urban Planning and Policy, so my focus is really on community development. I realized though, through my education and work, that there can be no development if we don't first develop the minds of our people. Because I am not a formal teacher, I have never been bound by any sort of formalities and rules that teachers may (or may not) have to follow. I work with youth on whatever level it takes to reach them. So, in the curriculum, you will notice that there are slang terms laced throughout. I know some people may say, "How can you teach job readiness using slang? These kids need to know how to talk right when they go into an interview." Well, my assumption is this: I've seen too many kids lost by a dry, "formal" curriculum that tries to be "right" because the creators are too detached from anything the kids can relate to. I have been most successful in my work because I can relate to them. Yeah, so it may not be "all that" to mix it up with a bit of "flava," but I would rather grab their attention from the get-go and keep them so they can get the lowdown on how to find a job and *then* work with them on how to "talk right." If you can't hang with the slang, this is probably not the curriculum that would suit you, and I have no issues with you for using something else. If you're looking for something new and fresh for your students, this may just be the curriculum you need, so keep reading to find out more information about it and this manual.

Tips for using *Your Promising Future* in class

Your Promising Future is not just a how-to-find-a-job workbook. Rather, it is a career development book that builds on itself. In the beginning, students are walked through activities that challenge them to think about what work really is and what it is that they really want to do in life. Then they are exposed to the feasibility and opportunities of postsecondary education. Before getting to the nitty-gritty how-to information on finding a job, students learn several necessary skills for leadership in their careers, and then they move on to the job search. By the end of the book, students will be fully prepared for their job search and career management.

When working with the students, I found it easiest to provide them as little information as possible through lectures. Lectures hold their attention for about five minutes—if you're good. Instead, I try to start each class with an icebreaker activity, an activity that leads into the topic of the day. Sometimes these icebreakers seem to have little relevance to the topic when the students begin, but there is always some connection between the icebreaker and that day's topic. Connecting the two creates a transition into the day's lecture. The lecture should be brief, often just 5–10 minutes, and should then lead into an activity, either one that is in the workbook or given in the *Your Promising Future Instructor's Guide.* Personally, I like to use the activities in the workbook as classroom activities and have the students complete the holla' zones as homework, but use the style that best fits your needs.

The *Your Promising Future Instructor's Guide* is really just a guide to give you some introductory activities, provide pre- and posttests and feedback forms, and fill you in on some teaching tips so you can look good during your performance. Truly the workbook is written in a very user-friendly manner and is very thorough, but it's always good to provide some human interaction in the learning process. That's where the real growing takes place, so relax, review, and prepare to have fun!

The *Your Promising Future* student workbook is filled with games, activities, real-life examples, and journaling-type components. It was designed so that students would think about life and what it is that they want out of it. Here are some tips to the various sections.

Administer a pretest and posttest after every chapter.

I suggest administering a pretest at the beginning of the chapter and then re-administering it as a posttest at the end of the chapter. You probably will want to grade the pretest but not count those grades toward their overall class grade. It is only to see how much the students know. If you want, you can return the tests so that the students can see what they missed. Then collect the pretests without discussing the answers.

At the end of the chapter, you can administer the same test as a posttest. However, you can expand on it by either writing additional questions or using some of the questions posted at the Web site for this book at www.jist.com.

I would keep all pretest questions at the beginning of a revised posttest. Then I could compare the questions from the pretest with the same questions on the posttest, showing the students how much improvement they made. When indicating the grades, I put two grades on the test–the pretest grade and the overall grade (which includes the pretest question score). When I returned the posttests, I handed back the pretests as well. Because I was using this curriculum as a WIA provider, I kept the pretest and posttest to prove growth and goal attainment.

The holla' zones are the students' turf.

The holla' zones are sections designed to let the students' thoughts flow freely. They are encouraged to not worry about how their responses come out. They are told to forget about whether

- their grammar is correct,
- they make sense, or
- their ideas sound crazy.

The students should have the freedom to just write what comes to them–what is on their hearts. I would suggest not grading these with letter grades based on content, but rather effort. I would always give students an "A" if they showed real effort in completing the section. I would give them a "C" if they did some work, but not much effort was put into it. If the section was not complete at all, they would obviously fail. Especially in the first few chapters, I would try to write questions to each student about what they wrote. These questions try to elicit more responses from the student, to get them to think more in depth on their response. Never criticize students for anything they write in these sections. If a student does get inappropriate, I do bring it to their attention, but in a very professional manner that tries to refocus them on the topic at hand–a positive future.

The Practice Makes Perfect sections call for accuracy.

Some activities in the book, though, such as the resume and application, are different. Students should fill these sections out with precision because they turn the forms in for a grade, and many can be used to find a job.

The rest of the book is for exploring who the students are.

For most of the other activities, the students shouldn't feel stressed to write certain responses. What is most important is that they figure out who they are. As with the holla' zones, many of the activities don't have right or wrong answers, so the students' grade should be based on effort. For maximum results using this curriculum, follow these tips:

- Integrate as many of the hands-on activities as possible into your classroom time.
- Have the students work in small groups as much as possible.
- Allow students to initiate discussions.
- Use as many different forms of media as possible. (Some suggestions are provided, but you will want to generate ideas on your own.)
- Ask the students to complete a feedback form after each chapter. You will find a generic feedback form at the back of the *Your Promising Future Instructor's Guide*.
- Bring in guest speakers.
- Follow the format: If you want to use only the job search section, that is okay, but for maximum results, work the curriculum from beginning to end.
- Involve students in mini-internships and have them present their experiences to the class.
- Take field trips to various businesses.
- Establish mentoring opportunities.
- Provide as much feedback as possible.
- When grading, rather than sticking to a formal scale, base grades on effort.
- Especially for the holla' zones, encourage the students to think critically by writing questions to them. Challenge them to think deeper as they're writing, but don't criticize their writing.
- At the end of Chapter 1, have a panel of business people from the community make a presentation on the impact of education on their lives to students. This presentation is most effective if you can find presenters who struggled while growing up but have become successful.
- By the end of Chapter 2, plan a field trip to a college fair or host one in the community.
- During Chapter 3, invite a community group to come in and present on issues such as gangs, violence, alcohol abuse, and so on.
- You may want to use the *Exploring Your Career Options* video from JIST Publishing with this course, as referenced in this guide.

All the best as you use this curriculum!

Meta

Got Game?

Creating a Game Plan for Your Life

1

Chapter Objectives

- Define the purpose of work
- Create a personal definition of success
- Recognize the benefit of volunteering as a means of learning about careers
- Take a career inventory
- Identify career interests

Introduction

This chapter leads students through activities that will help them discover their skills, interests, and dreams—all keys to opening up their minds to finding a career that suits who they are. They are challenged to re-think their own notions of what work is and to define their own careers. They will also learn about the sacrifices it takes to achieve goals.

Classroom Configurations

The classroom setup varies from session to session. I recommend that the desks are in a circle or semicircle rather than in rows. I generally try to start the classes with a whole-class activity or an activity involving small groups of two or three. Using activities gets the students involved in that day's topic in a hands-on way, engaging their attention right away.

Chapter Outline

Topic I.   Life: The Most Important Game You'll Play

        A. Who Says Work Has to Be Boring?

        B. Your Dreams Can Become Real

        C. Hard Work and Sacrifice Get You There

        D. Don't Let Fear Hold You Back

Topic II.   What Does Success Mean to You?

        A. Success Isn't for Chickens or the Lazy

        B. Create Your Own Definition of Success

C. Mission Accomplished: Find Purpose in Work

Topic III. Volunteering: A Way to Discover Life

A. Discover the Difference You Can Make

B. Find Your Volunteering Destination

Topic IV. Be Whatcha Wanna Be

A. Let Your Interests Be Your Career Guide

B. You're Sure to Find a Career That Fits You

C. Be True to Your Values When Deciding on a Career

D. Seek and You Will Find Ways to Turn Your Dreams into a Career

Presentation Plan

The following section illustrates my methods of presenting the material to students, incorporating the activities found in the *Your Promising Future* workbook. You will want to adapt the methods and schedule to meet the needs of your students and situation.

Introduction Introduce the program very briefly. Explain that the program will be addressing career and educational issues in a hands-on manner and that you will begin with a game.

Notes/Tips   Rather than spending a lot of time talking about what this class has to offer, just do a brief introduction for the class, and jump right into the game.

              I normally begin by introducing the instructor(s) and saying, "This class is designed to help you make career decisions for your life in a fun and hands-on manner. Rather than just tell you about what the class has to offer, let's play a game to find out. But first take this pretest to see what you already know."

Pretest Hand out a short quiz to test the students' knowledge of the content before the presentation. (See the "Chapter 1 Test" section.)

Icebreaker 1: Career Jeopardy A game that introduces the staff and program and makes the students feel relaxed.

Objective   Demonstrate teamwork

Materials   Magnetic board, game pieces, poster board, PowerPoint slide, and prizes

Procedure   1. Divide the class into several teams.

                 2. Go over rules.

                 3. Play "Promising Futures Jeopardy," found in the "Suggestions and Teaching Tips" section.

                 4. After the game, tally up the points and give out prizes to the winning team.

                 5. Award prizes accordingly.

Session One

Rules	1. Any team member can answer because the points go to the team.
	2. Raise hand to respond.
	3. Answer in the form of a question.
	4. The time limit is three seconds.
Time	10–25 minutes
Notes/Tips	After giving prizes, debrief and provide more detail on the program.

Possible Script:

> This game was just a brief introduction to the many issues we will be working with to better prepare you for setting goals that will allow you to succeed not only in school, but in life. Some of the topics we will be addressing in these sessions are
>
> Education options after high school
>
> Financial aid–how to get it
>
> Networking
>
> How to find the right job that fits your interests
>
> Job search skills
>
> What employers look for
>
> Resume writing
>
> Interviewing
>
> Goal setting
>
> Leadership skills
>
> Please remember: Even though this work is graded, the most important thing for you to understand is that this class is designed to provide you with tools to succeed in life.
>
> The objective of this curriculum is to be fun and informative, so you will be working in groups, playing games, and thinking without even knowing it.

You may want to use the PowerPoint slide "Your Promising Future: What You'll Learn" here.

This activity may take the whole first session, without giving time to really meet the students. To save time, I had students sign in on attendance sheets and didn't spend time taking attendance. At the end of the class, state that you want to learn more about them, but that will be done next class. Ask them to think about what it is that they want to do in life and come up with a personal philosophy–a phrase or quotation that describes them, such as "never give up" (which is mine).

(continues)

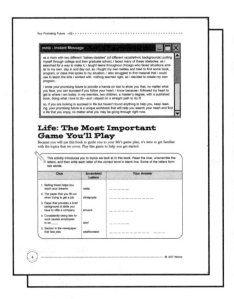

Session One

(continued)

Homework: Scrambled Words This word scramble presents the topics addressed in the course.

Objectives	Develop critical thinking skills
	Introduce students to topics in the book
Materials	Worksheet and pencil
Procedure	1. Read the clue.
	2. Unscramble the letters.
	3. Write each letter of the correct word on the blank line.
Notes/Tips	Have the students do the word scramble to fill time or as homework.

Session Two

Introduction In this session, we will be looking at work and what that really means. Can work be fun? Let's find out. First, let's get to know each other a little more.

Icebreaker 2: I'd Like to Introduce Myself An activity in which everyone learns students' names and interests and practices being supportive of others' career interests.

Objectives	Demonstrate the proper way of introducing one's self
	Recognize the situations in which people work together rather than competitively
Materials	Soft ball or object to toss around
Procedure	1. Form a circle.
	2. Tell the students to toss the ball softly.
	3. The instructor states his or her name, future plans, and personal philosophy.
	4. The instructor throws the ball to a student.
	5. The student introduces self and throws the ball to another student.
	6. The process continues until all have introduced themselves.
Rule	Toss the ball gently to the next student, making it easily caught.
Time	10–15 minutes
Notes/Tips	Here is an example of a personal philosophy: When I do this program, I introduce my name and plans and state that my personal philosophy is "never give up." A personal philosophy should be a phrase that a person lives by, that motivates him or her, etc. Make sure that it is short and to the point. Make sure that students come up with something. They should not get away with "I don't know."

If possible, try to keep notes about the students. I like to keep attendance by having a sign-in sheet, so I take an extra sign-in sheet and write down the students' responses on the signature line.

Activity: Who Says Work Has to Be Boring? Create a positive definition and image of work so students learn that work can be more than just a means to get money; it can be an expression of interests, beliefs, and values.

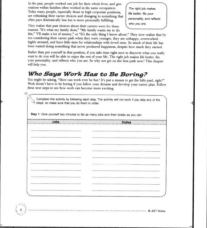

Objectives	Compare personal interest level in two different activities
	Recognize the impact that interest and aptitude have on career choices
Materials	Markers, two bottles of glue, six scissors, newsprint, work-related magazines, prizes, and lined paper
Procedure	1. Divide the class into two groups.
	2. Give each group instructions.
	3. Complete the project.
	4. Groups report to the class.
Rules	1. Group 1 instructions: Your job is to write individual lists of jobs and the duties of each. You are not allowed to work with anyone else. You will be "paid" for the length and quality of your list, so work hard and do a good job.
	2. Group 2 instructions: Your job is to work as a group and come up with a creative way to describe as many different careers as you can think of. You could draw something, make a collage, write a song, or do any combination of things to present the information. The entire group will be paid based on the final product.
Time	10 minutes for activity, 15 minutes for discussion
Notes/Tips	There will probably be a lot of complaining and maybe some noncompliance from Group 1, which is good. The intent of this group is to show how people often work in jobs that are mundane and they don't enjoy, but they do it for the money. Find some sort of payment for those who put effort into the work for each group.
	When the time is up, ask students in Group 1 to tally up the number of jobs they were able to come up with. While they are doing that, one of the instructors will tell the class what each group had to do.
	Ask Group 1, "Who came up with the most jobs and descriptions?" Have the top two people read their lists. Next, have Group 2 present their project.

(continues)

(continued)

Then ask each group, starting with Group 1:

How did you feel about your project?

Was it fun? Boring?

Did it feel like work?

Was it something you wanted to do?

Why did you choose (or not choose) to do it?

After both groups have responded, give "payment" and then debrief.

Review: Most people view work as Group 1 did—not excited. They just do it for the money because they want something, like those "things" from the icebreaker. The reality is that what Group 2 did was also work as they accomplished the same task. Yet, Group 2 was (hopefully) much more interested in the project because they accomplished the task by using skills and talents that they enjoyed using. In life, if we pick our jobs based on skills and talents, we will be much happier in our jobs and can often incorporate those "things" we want into our jobs. Even if we don't get the things we want, we are still happy because we are doing things we enjoy.

Activity: holla' zone Students write about their dreams.

Materials	Worksheet and pencil
Notes/Tips	Encourage students to be creative in this—not to worry about what anyone might think or say. Just write down dreams they have had, whether they still think about doing those things or not. It may be helpful if you come up with some examples from your own life—things you have never done, but think about doing, knowing that they may or may not happen. When you show the students that you can put yourself out there and be open, they are more willing to open up with you.
Time	10 minutes

Video The "Show Me the Money" section in the bonus content following the video *Exploring Your Career Options* works well with this session.

Session Three

Introduction In this session, students work more on realizing their dreams and thinking of ways to turn them into work.

Icebreaker 3: Guided Imagery This activity introduces students to a positive definition and image of work.

Objective	Recognize that work can be positive
Materials	Guided imagery script:

> Close your eyes and think back to a time when you were little. Think back to that moment you were watching TV or reading a book and you heard about the most fascinating thing. It may have been about traveling to some-place new, it may have been about someone's job, it may have been about a sports team or a person winning some sort of award. Whatever it was, it lit you up inside. Your smile was so big that even your eyes began to smile inside, and something made you say, "I want to do that!"

Procedure	1. Hand out paper.
	2. Explain the guided imagery exercise.
	3. Read the guided imagery script.
	4. Ask students to write down what lit them up inside.
	5. Have a few students share their responses.
	6. Ask students if and why they (or some people) stopped believing they could have that thing.
Time	10 minutes
Notes/Tips	Many students who have done this activity say they don't believe they could have these things. Common responses were due to minority status, economic status, gender, etc. Also common is "I see how hard my parents work, and they hardly make anything. I'll end up with the same type of job, in the same situation." The root of all these responses is money, so the intent of the session is to question how people get money (which generally is work) and to (re)define the meaning of work. This should be done before the students do the workbook, as it will help them come up with ideas for the activity.

Video The introduction to the video *Exploring Your Career Options* ties in nicely with the next activity.

(continues)

Session Three

(continued)

Activity: Your Dreams Can Become Real Students identify their personal goals and dreams.

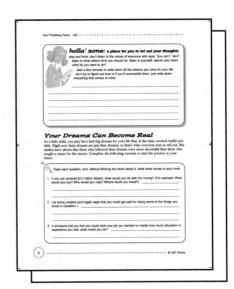

Objective	Identify dreams and goals
Materials	Worksheet, paper, and pencil
Procedure	1. Allow 10 minutes for each student to complete the worksheet.
	2. Pair students up.
	3. Students go over their responses with their partners.
	4. Have the pair come up with a business idea that incorporates the two dreams together and write it down on paper.
	5. Share the "joint ventures" from each group with the class.
Time	25 minutes
Notes/Tips	When students pair up and work on their "joint venture," encourage them to think creatively. You may get someone who wants to do mechanical work with a fashion designer, but that is okay. The students need to come up with a business design and describe what the business would do, who it would serve, and some products or services that the business would offer.

Session Four

Introduction Dreams don't just happen. You can always have what you want. You just have to be willing to pay the price to get it, which means hard work and sacrifice. This can be a bit scary and look intimidating, but when you set your sights to reach your goals and give up those things that will hinder your progress, anything is possible.

Icebreaker 4: Break Out Students watch a demonstration of what it takes to accomplish your goals.

Objectives	Identify fears
	Recognize how to overcome obstacles and fears to reach goals
Materials	Three volunteers, four pillow-like balls, and prizes
Procedure	1. Select three students to participate in the following demonstration, and make sure that there is plenty of space to move at the front of the room.
	2. Choose one student for each of the following roles:
	goal setter
	attacker
	retriever of the balls

3. Place the prize at one end of the room and tell the goal setter that, in order to receive the prize, he or she must walk to the other end of the room to get it.

4. While the person is going to the other side, the attacker throws balls, trying to knock him or her off course. (Stress that the balls cannot be thrown very hard and avoid hitting the head.)

5. The retriever catches the balls and throws them back to the attacker.

6. The goal setter can choose to decline the offer or accept. If he declines, he doesn't get the prize. If he accepts, he must go for the prize and "dodge the bullets" being thrown at him.

7. When someone accepts the prize, discuss the activity with the class.

Time	7 minutes
Notes/Tips	As this demonstration shows, when you go after your goals, obstacles will come up to stop you. If you look at the obstacles and become intimidated, you will never reach the prize. If you take the risk and go for it, you will get your prize. Even if the person was hit with the ball, the hit didn't injure him. It may have startled him for a second and slowed him down, but he got back up and kept going. That's how life is. There will be plenty of things to knock you off your course, but when you are determined and keep trying, you can have what you go for.

The following quotes may be useful in this session:

> *"I trust so much in the power of the heart and the soul; I know that the answer to what we need to do next is in our own hearts. All we have to do is listen, then take that one step further and trust what we hear. We will be taught what we need to learn."*
>
> *– Melody Beattie*

> *"Ultimately, we must learn to trust ourselves. When we do this intimately and intelligently, the world opens full of meaning before us. We find that we ourselves are the doorway to a fathomless understanding of the source of life itself. We need only to learn to walk through it."*
>
> *– James Thornton*

(continues)

(continued)

Activities: Hard Work and Sacrifice Will Get You There and **Don't Let Fear Hold You Back** Students decide what they are willing to sacrifice to make their dreams come true.

Objectives	Recognize personal fears that may hinder success
	Evaluate the role of choice in determining one's future
Materials	Worksheets and pencil
Procedure	1. Students complete both worksheets on their own. Allow no more than 10 minutes for this.
	2. The students get in groups of threes.
	3. Each group should discuss the realities of these sacrifices and fears (how easy it is to just forget what everyone else says, not look at the financial responsibilities, etc.).
	4. The students present their discussion.
Time	30 minutes
Notes/Tips	Try to pull out some positive things that students can do to overcome the obstacles. Don't just let them settle for "Yeah, this stuff sounds good, but it won't work because. . ." Have them generate ideas on how to make it work. A possible suggestion, depending on the outcome of the discussion, could be this: If there is a policy, rule, or system that seems to be failing the students or could use some changes, have the students write letters to the administration in these areas, whether it be the school, community, government, and so on.

Activity: holla' zone Students analyze information presented in this section and make a personal conclusion.

Materials	Worksheet and pencil
Time	10 minutes

Session Four

Introduction In this session, students create their personal definition of success, something that they can carry with them in life.

Icebreaker 5: What Does Success Mean to You? Students write down their opinions about what success means.

Objectives	Identify signs of success
	Draw conclusions about the source of personal values
Materials	Worksheet and pen
Procedure	1. Go over the directions in the workbook.
	2. Give students three minutes to write as many definitions as they can think of.
	3. The students pair up. Give three more minutes to come up with new ideas.
	4. Pairs of students get with another pair. Give three more minutes to share what they came up with or come up with any new ideas.
	5. Do a group review, asking some of the questions in the notes/tips section.
Time	15 minutes
Notes/Tips	After the students have done group work, have them stay in their group. If they would like, they can select a group spokesperson, or anyone from the group can comment. Engage the class in a discussion. Use following questions as a guide:

Where did your original beliefs come from?

Did you have any of the same beliefs as your partner?

Did any of your beliefs differ?

What were some major differences between your beliefs?

How did this activity change your view of what success could be?

Activity: holla' zone Students are given two scenarios and asked to decide which doctor is the more successful.

Objective	Transfer definition of success to new situations
Materials	Flip chart, marker, and worksheet
Procedure	1. Select one student to read the scenario in the holla' zone.
	2. Ask the students which doctor they think is more successful.
	3. Divide the students into two groups—one chooses the rich doctor as successful; and the other, the community doctor.

(continues)

(continued)

4. The students do one of two things:

- List reasons why they believe what they believe and have a short debate. If they choose this option, each point should be recorded on the flip chart (make sure to denote which doctor each point is for).

- Each group debates or comes up with reasons why the other doctor is successful (that is, they have to reverse their stance and argue for it).

5. Close with the "right" answer; either doctor could be considered successful provided they are doing what they love and helping others.

Time   30 minutes

Notes/Tips   After this session, go over the definitions of success and lead the students into the homework worksheets (see the following two worksheets).

Homework: Success Isn't for Chickens or the Lazy Students interview a successful person and draw conclusions about success.

Objectives   Identify a successful person

Conduct an interview

Draw conclusions about that person's success

Procedure   Ask students to take this activity home and do it as homework because it requires interviewing another person. You may need to give up to a week for this.

Homework: Create Your Own Definition of Success
Students write individual definitions of success. They gain the most by doing this activity alone.

Objectives   Integrate knowledge gained from class and interviewing in developing a definition of success

Apply definition of success to future goals

Materials   Workbook and pencil

Procedure

1. Generate class discussion asking this question: When will you know that you have become successful?

2. After a brief discussion, have the students work on their charts in the workbook. This will probably become homework.

Notes/Tips

If students don't understand the question or are not very responsive, suggest the following ideas (and come up with more):

Having enough money to get the things you need/want

Reaching your goals

Improving your life (Example: You lived in public housing, but now have your own house)

Being famous

Having a degree

You may want to use the PowerPoint slide on success here.

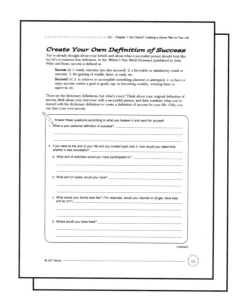

Session Six

Introduction Students learn more about volunteering and how it can help to develop their career paths.

Icebreaker 6: Where to Go Students brainstorm about places where they can volunteer.

Objectives

Identify places to volunteer

Recognize the value of volunteering in developing career paths

Materials

Paper, pencil, and topics (see icebreaker section)

Procedure

1. The students form four groups.

2. Pass out a topic to each group, using these topics:

Park	Hospital
Museum	Nursing home
Zoo	Library
Theater	Wildlife refuge
Church	Botanical garden

(continues)

(continued)

3. Give the students five minutes to come up with as many different places as they know about (local, statewide, national, or international) that focus on that topic.

4. Students share their responses with the class at the end of the activity.

Time   10 minutes

Notes/Tips   After the icebreaker, go over the PowerPoint slide about mission finding. Talk about ways to discover jobs that match their interests.

Activity: Discover the Difference You Can Make

This activity taps into the students' interests as a part of discovering potential careers.

Objectives   Apply information about volunteering to personal life

              Recognize personal roles in citizenship

Materials   Worksheet and pencil

Procedure   1. Students complete the worksheet alone.

              2. Use this worksheet to complete the next activity.

Time   10 minutes

Notes/Tips   Students should complete this activity fairly rapidly and go on to the Internet.

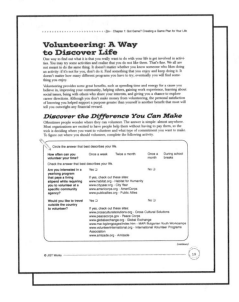

Activity: Find Your Volunteering Destination

Students research volunteer opportunities.

Objective   Demonstrate ability to use the Internet to research specific volunteer programs

Materials   Internet, worksheet, pencil, and PowerPoint slide of Volunteering resources

Procedure   1. Students get on the Internet.

              2. Display the PowerPoint slide of resources for students to check out.

              3. Students select a Web site to check out (either from the slide, the examples in the worksheet, or by doing a keyword search on the Internet) and research an organization they could volunteer with.

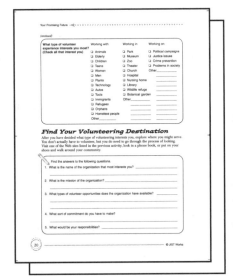

4. Students complete the worksheet.

5. Four or five students share what they learned.

Time	25 minutes
Notes/Tips	To add some variation to your classroom, before or after this activity, invite someone from one of the volunteer groups—such as Public Allies, AmeriCorps, or so on—to make a class presentation. Or ask students who have volunteered to discuss their experiences.

Homework: holla' zone Students integrate their knowledge of volunteering with their personal values.

Materials	Worksheet and pencil
Notes/Tips	This should be done as homework, but if students finish the previous activity, they can begin working on this to fill time. Responses could be shared in a class discussion.

Introduction In the next few sessions, students look more into careers that match their interests and research specific careers.

Icebreaker 7: Be Whatcha Wanna Be Students match careers with their descriptions and salaries.

Objective	Understand that careers differ in responsibilities and compensations
Materials	Pre-written index cards and prizes
Procedure	1. From the Be Whatcha Wanna Be answer key, take the job titles and their descriptions and salaries and put them on index cards.

2. Divide the students into two groups. One group of students will be "Jobs," and the others will be "Job descriptions."

3. Each student receives an index card that will have listed either a job or a job description, depending on what group they are.

4. The students go around the room and talk to each other to find out who is the other half of their pair. They should keep in mind that the jobs that are being used for this activity are most likely not your typical job, so they shouldn't be surprised by the descriptions.

5. Award prizes to the three fastest pairs with the correct answers.

Time	10 minutes

(continues)

Session Seven

(continued)

Notes/Tips   When many people think of jobs, they think of common jobs, such as retail, banking, factory work, teaching, and so on. Many of the jobs people think of are on a 9-to-5 type timetable and often don't allow for creativity, or at least people think that. The reality is that there are more than 22,000 occupations in America and many different ways to accomplish tasks. We cannot let what is seen dictate what we know about work because most of what these students– and many people–see about work is just the tip of the iceberg. If anyone wants to truly succeed and do what they really enjoy doing, they must seek out information. This session is just a taste of some of the different jobs that are out there. The hope is that the students are encouraged to look at work in a new way and seek out some way to integrate their skills and interests with a job.

Activity: Let Your Interests Be Your Guide Students go through a career inventory and highlight careers and career categories that interest them.

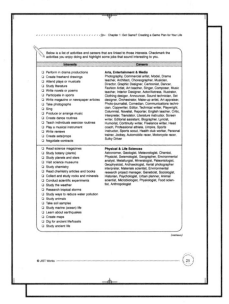

Objective   Recognize personal career interests

Materials   Worksheet and pencil

Procedure   1. Turn to the appropriate page in the workbook.

2. Students highlight or circle activities that they enjoy (or think they may enjoy) doing in each category.

3. Students highlight or circle careers that correspond with those interests for each category.

4. If they aren't interested in any careers in the box, do not circle any.

5. Add up the number of interests in each box. The highest number denotes which career area they would most likely look for a job in.

Time   25 minutes

Notes/Tips   When the students go over the lists, let them know that they can circle activities that they think would interest them, even if they have not yet done them.

Also, make sure they circle careers that sound interesting to them, even if they don't know much about them.

If you want to use a different inventory, JIST Publishing has a variety of inventories to choose from; visit their Web site (www.jist.com) or call them at 1-800-648-JIST. One that I have used in the past is the Career Exploration Inventory. The staff at JIST is very helpful when you call and could recommend one that would fit your student profile most appropriately.

Video The chapter points "What Are Your Interests?" and "Tools to a Career" in *Exploring Your Career Options* are an excellent way to close this session.

Introduction In this session, students explore ways to match their interests with their values as well as other jobs that are out there. They are challenged to think beyond just the jobs they know and research new possibilities.

Icebreaker 8: Career Toss Students write out their dreams and have classmates provide input on ways to turn those dreams into a career.

Objectives	Recognize personal interests
	Apply knowledge of careers to current situations
Materials	Paper and pencil
Procedure	1. Everyone sits down–desks in a semicircle.
	2. Students list their top three favorite things to do on a piece of paper.
	3. They crumple up the paper and throw it to the middle of the room (or you could have them make it into a paper airplane and say "watch your dreams soar" and ask them to send the airplane to the middle).
	4. Pick up someone else's paper.
	5. On the paper, write down three jobs that fit each interest.
	6. The students fold/crumple the paper and send them to the middle again and repeat the last two steps.
	7. Four students share what was written on their paper.
Time	10 minutes
Notes/Tips	I always thought it would be great to have the students put their names on the paper, but I also didn't want any student to be embarrassed to write anything. You know your students. If they do put their names on their papers, the papers should be returned to them and then a few students could share what was written on their papers. I think it would be wonderful for students to see what other people come up with.
	As a transition to the worksheet, you can talk about how there are many jobs that may fit your interests. It is just a matter of learning about what is out there and matching your interests to those careers.

Activity: You're Sure to Find a Career That Fits Your Interest Students research careers on the Internet.

Objectives	Research careers in their field that they don't know much about
	Demonstrate that they have broadened their career horizons
Materials	Worksheet, pencil, and the Internet

(continues)

Session Eight

(continued)

Procedure
1. The students choose two jobs from their dominant career field from the previous activity that they know little about and would like to explore.

2. On the Internet, go to the http://stats.bls.gov/oco Web site.

3. Students research the jobs they have selected and complete the worksheet.

4. Students present their findings.

Time
30 minutes

Notes/Tips
After this project (or you could wait until Session Ten), you could have the students arrange a career fair to present information about the careers they have researched.

Session Nine

Introduction Students match their interests, desires, and values with a career. It is important to know that no job meets all our needs and desires. If we know what sort of work environment works best for us, we are much happier in our jobs even if it isn't exactly what we wanted. Being able to define interests and values will help students in their career searches.

Icebreaker 9: Be True to Your Values Students complete the worksheet to discover work environments that are suitable for them.

Objective
Identify personal values and what you would like in a job

Materials
Worksheet and pencil

Procedure
1. Students select a partner.

2. Students complete the worksheet independently and discuss their answers with their partner.

3. The pair comes up with an "ideal" job for each other—whether it's a real job out there right now or not.

4. A few groups share with the class.

Time
6 minutes

Notes/Tips
Encourage the students to be creative and let their minds flow when doing this activity. Encourage them not to focus just on the jobs they know about when describing an ideal job. Even when I do this activity for myself, I go over what I like and don't like to do and then I try to find a job that suits that. I have even created (or worked with employers to create) that reality for myself.

Activity: The Wide World of Work Students watch videos that illustrate the point that work can be more than just a means to get money; it can be an expression of a person's interests, beliefs, and values.

Objective	Recognize that a myriad of careers are available to those who can't "get with" a traditional job
Materials	Worksheet and pencil
Procedure	1. Make a worksheet with the following questions for each job that you want to focus on: (These are not in the workbook.)

What does the person(s) do?

What sort of educational background does he or she have?

How did he or she get involved in this job?

What sort of advice does he or she give on finding a job?

What are some benefits of the job?

What does the person enjoy most about the job?

2. Show as many of the following videos as desired.

3. Students complete worksheets either during or after video.

4. Discuss this activity as a class.

Notes/Tips Listed are videos that I chose in which the people discuss how they took a common interest they had and turned it into a career that they enjoy. In addition, each person discusses steps to success and provides words of encouragement that are helpful to youth. These videos are in a series of 50 videos, so they are not the only ones to choose from. Because I have worked with a variety of inner-city youth, I looked for videos that best related to them. There may be other videos more appropriate for your students, either through this company or another, but remember that you may have to rework some of the worksheet if you use other videos. I tried to show as many of the segments as possible. You may choose only one or two, or all; it's up to you.

Here is the information for the videos:

Media Pro 888-661-8104

$60 each + shipping and handling

Real Life 101: Volume 1–Sporting Events Coordinator

Real Life 101: Volume 1–FUBU Clothing Designers

Real Life 101: Volume 12–Lego Designer

Real Life 101: Volume 12–Pyrotechnician

Real Life 101: Volume 12–Personal Trainer

Video The section "Do You Want to Be the Next Big Sports Star?" in the bonus content following *Exploring Your Career Options* is appropriate here or at the beginning of Session Ten.

Introduction This day should be devoted to the library for research. Students will be doing a more extensive research on a career that interests them. There is no icebreaker for this day. You should probably plan to have the students meet you in the library.

Homework: Seek and You Will Find Ways to Turn Your Dreams into a Career Students research career opportunities and educational requirements.

Objective	Research the various career paths in a specific field of interest
Materials	Library books, worksheet, pencil, and library
Procedure	1. Meet in the library.
	2. Go over the instructions.
	3. Students find materials about a profession they are interested in.
	4. Students fill out the worksheet.
	5. Students check out any materials that are necessary to complete the assignment.
	6. Students write a report on their findings.
	7. Discuss their findings as a class.
Time	Entire session and homework (may give up to a week to complete)
Notes/Tips	This may be the appropriate place for the students to put together a "career day" in which they present their findings. They could consider contacting different companies that are affiliated with that field to get literature, create a poster board presentation, etc.

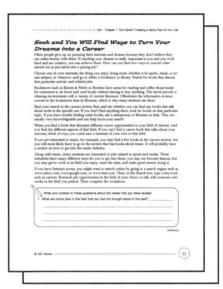

Activity: holla' zone Students should do this writing assignment alone, describing a personal response to the information presented in this chapter.

Materials	Worksheet and pencil
Time	10 minutes

Posttest Hand out a short quiz to test the students' knowledge of the content after the presentation. (See the "Chapter 1 Test" section.)

Materials	Form and pencil
Time	10 minutes

Feedback Using the template in the back of this guide, create a feedback form that gives the students an opportunity to react emotionally and intellectually to the information presented in this chapter.

Materials	Form and pencil
Time	10 minutes

Suggestions and Teaching Tips

It is very important to address critical-thinking skills used in this chapter, especially in the holla' zone sections. The activities throughout the book require these skills. If they aren't fostered from the beginning, it will be difficult to keep the students engaged.

Also, it is important to remember not to grade the holla' zones based on grammar, but rather on content. Additionally, make comments or ask questions to encourage students to write more in these sections. I know doing so takes extra time to grade, but if you do it in the beginning, the students will respond. It will be easier for you to grade in the long run, and the students will benefit more from the book. Often I have found that kids are not taught/expected/asked to think critically, so it may be difficult to get them to open up at first. But if you set the stage from the beginning and keep enforcing it, it will come.

Promising Future Jeopardy Game Board

Below is the game board for the Promising Future Jeopardy game. You will need to supply clues for the Instructors column. Make a copy for each group.

Promising Future Jeopardy			
Promising Futures	**Instructors**	**Job Search**	**Education**
100	**100**	**100**	**100**
The number of years this program has been at this school	The names of the instructors	The paper that one fills out when he/she is trying to get a job	What everyone should obtain to help get a better-paying job or enlist in the armed services
200	**200**	**200**	**200**
The two main issues that will be addressed by the Promising Futures program		The conversation between an employer and potential employee necessary for obtaining employment	One way to get money for college; BONUS 100 POINTS if you can name two other ways to get money for college
300	**300**	**300**	**300**
The method for delivery of the program		Two ways to gain work experience without getting paid	The name of the application one fills out to qualify for financial aid
400	**400**	**400**	**400**
The year this program was created		This job search technique is cited as the most effective way to find a job	The type of schooling one seeks out to prepare for a specific skilled occupation

Promising Futures Jeopardy Answers

Below are the answers for the Promising Futures Jeopardy game. Because you are supplying some of the information, you will also need to supply some of the answers in the Promising Futures and Instructors columns.

Promising Futures	Instructors	Job Search	Education
100	**100**	**100**	**100**
The number of years this program has been at this school **(Answer varies)**	The names of the instructors **(Answer varies, depending on the instructors' names)**	The paper that one fills out when he/she is trying to get a job **(Application)**	What everyone should obtain to help get a better-paying job or enlist in the armed services **(Diploma)**
200	**200**	**200**	**200**
The two main issues that will be addressed by the Promising Futures program **(Education and careers)**	**(Answer varies, depending on the instructor clue inserted in the game board)**	The conversation between an employer and potential employee necessary for obtaining employment **(Interviewing)**	One way to get money for college; BONUS 100 POINTS if you can name two other ways to get money for college **(Loans, grants, scholarships, work study)**
300	**300**	**300**	**300**
The method for delivery of the program **(Hands-on)**	**(Answer varies, depending on the instructor clue inserted in the game board)**	Two ways to gain work experience without getting paid **(Internships and volunteering)**	The name of the application one fills out to qualify for financial aid **(FAFSA)**
400	**400**	**400**	**400**
The year this program was created **(Varies)**	**(Answer varies, depending on the instructor clue inserted in the game board)**	This job search technique is cited as the most effective way to find a job **(Networking)**	The type of schooling one seeks out to prepare for a specific skilled occupation **(Trade school)**

Icebreaker 7 Be Whatcha Wanna Be Entries

You can copy the following table and then cut each section apart to create the index cards.

Veterinary technician	Assist in caring for animals, collect specimens, and assist in surgery. Salary: $18,000–$35,000
Event planner	Develop themes for events, choose sites, negotiate contracts, and book entertainment. Salary: $20,000–$150,000+
Geriatric care manager	Serve as stand-in relative, pay bills, make appointments, and visit clients as needed. Salary: $25,000–$85,000+
Copywriter	Write effective, creative copy for print ads, TV and radio commercials, and brochures. Salary: $23,000–$100,000
Radio/TV advertising salesperson	Sell space to advertisers for commercials. Salary: $20,000–$125,000
Dance therapist	Use dance to treat physical, mental, or emotional habits. Salary: $22,000–$55,000+
Publicity consultant	Obtain publicity, write press releases, and talk with media. Salary: $20,000–150,000+
Music therapist	Treat physical, mental, or emotional disabilities with the help of music. Salary: $19,000–$48,000
Environmental engineer	Supervise cleanup of contamination and design environmentally safe systems. Salary: $35,000–$100,000
Personal shopper	Coordinate colors, styles, and fabrics for customers; offer opinions about merchandise. Salary: $24,000–$68,000+
Private investigator	Perform background checks, conduct surveillance, search for missing people. Salary: $20,000–$85,000+
Caterer	Prepare food for parties, home meals, and events; serve food; develop themes. Salary: $20,000–$90,000+
Computer and software trainer	Train individuals to use computers, develop curriculum, and answer questions. Salary: $23,000–$55,000
Personal trainer	Plan and supervise fitness regimes for clients on a one-on-one basis. Pay: $35–$750 per session
Technical documentation specialist	Prepare materials, write online help, put technical information into everyday language. Salary: $25,000–$70,000+
Advertising art director	Design advertisements, including graphics, layout, and artwork. Salary: $18,000–$100,000
Dietician	Design diets, promote healthful eating habits, research nutritional needs. Salary: $25,000–$70,000+

Class Topics and Discussions

If you have a few free minutes or if you're having trouble engaging the students or you know of particular situations in the lives of the students that could benefit from discussion, you may want to initiate a discussion of any or all of these topics:

● Why do people move from their home countries to the United States? What do they gain? What do they lose?

● Do you want to support your family the same way one of your parents have? Why or why not?

● Should parents expect their adult children to take over the family business when the parents die or can no longer work?

● How can you tell whether a dream or goal is worth your effort?

● Describe a time when you or someone you know sacrificed to achieve a goal. Was the sacrifice worthwhile?

● Describe a time when you overcame or helped someone overcome fear. Was the effort worthwhile?

● Why do most people choose the jobs they have? Or why does or do your parent(s) work the jobs they do?

● Why should we care about how our careers impact the lives of others?

● How can the work you do within your community affect the world on a global level?

● What role does politics play in determining who works in what types of jobs?

● Should illegal immigrants be allowed to work?

● Are laws written to help people succeed? fail?

● Should college be offered free of charge?

PowerPoint Slides

I have prepared several PowerPoint slides to accompany this chapter and present them here as pages that you can copy to hand out, convert to transparencies, or scan to create PowerPoint presentations. However, if you would like to have the actual PowerPoint slides, please contact your JIST representative at 1-800-648-5478 or check out our Web site at www.jist.com.

Your Promising Future

What You'll Learn

- Discover your dreams

- Set goals for your life

- Develop leadership skills

- Weave your skills into a career

To give of one's self, to leave the world a bit better, whether by a healthy child, a garden patch or a redeemed social condition; to have played and laughed with enthusiasm and sung with exultation; to know that even one life has breathed easier because you have lived—that is to have succeeded.

--Ralph Waldo Emerson

How to Find Your Mission

1. <u>Seek</u> out the type of work that your heart is drawn to.

2. <u>Find</u> a way to do what you love to make a positive contribution in the world.

3. <u>Engage</u> in activities to see where you truly fit in.

A Few Web Sites for Volunteering

❑ www.bmf.net — Black media foundation

❑ www.americorps.org — AmeriCorps

❑ www.crossculturalsolutions.org — Cross Cultural Solutions

❑ www.globalvolunteers.org — Global Volunteers, Partners in Development

❑ www.idealist.org — Idealist and Action Without Borders

❑ www.pointsoflight.org — Points of Light Foundation

❑ www.servenet.org — Web site for service and for volunteering

❑ www.volunteerinternational.org — An up-to-date search site for international volunteer and internship opportunities

❑ www.youthforanimals.org — Youth Corps for Animals

Outside Class Activities and Homework

What do you do if you know that your message isn't getting through to one of your students? Why don't you try a different approach? In this section, I offer a few suggestions that focus on the visual, auditory, and kinesthetic learning styles. Let my suggestions just be a starting point for you, though. Use your imagination, creativity, and knowledge of your students to come up with even more effective methods of communicating the message.

Topics	Learning Styles		
	Visual	**Auditory**	**Kinesthetic**
Attitudes toward work	Create a collage showing people at work.	Write a rap about attitudes toward work.	Create and perform a mime act or dance.
Inspiring stories taken from religious, political, sports, or entertainment heroes	Write a brief biographical essay or a play about someone you admire who overcame obstacles and became a success.	Find and bring to class a song or story that illustrates someone overcoming or giving in to obstacles.	Create a game of charades based on the names of famous overcomers.
Dreams	Create a collage showing what you'd like to have in your future.	Tape little children describing the goals they have for their lives.	Build a model of the home or office you'd like to have be part of your future.
Fears that hold people back from success	Make 4 or 5 small posters that inspire others to overcome fears.	Create some cheers, a rap, or a song that encourages others to overcome fears.	Build a mobile or sculpture that illustrates fears.

Chapter 1 Test

I always give a pretest as a way of introducing students to the upcoming topics and discovering what they already know. I do not discuss the answers on the pretest. I then administer the same test as a posttest, discussing the answers within the same class period.

In Appendix B, you will find additional questions you may want to use, depending upon the requirements for the sessions that you're teaching.

Name _____

Date _____

Chapter 1 Your Promising Future

Please take the time to fill this out. If you don't know the answer to a question, you may write "I don't know."

1. What is your instructor's name?_____

2. What is *Your Promising Future*? _____

    _____

    _____

3. How can *Your Promising Future* help you? _____

    _____

    _____

4. What career category do you fall into? _____

    _____

    _____

5. What do you want to be when you grow up and why? _____

    _____

    _____

    _____

6. What is the best way for you to learn new information? (This question has no right or wrong answer. It is about you personally.)

    _____

    _____

    _____

    _____

    _____

    _____

    _____

    _____

    _____

    _____

    _____

Chapter 1 Your Promising Future Answers

1. Answers will vary.

2. A course of study that helps students define their goals, dreams, and future career.

3. Answers will vary.

4. Answers will vary.

5. Answers will vary.

6. Answers will vary.

Resources

Following are some videos, Web sites, and books that you may find helpful. Remember that Web site addresses frequently change. If a site is no longer active, try using a search engine to locate the organization's current Web site.

Resources for Videos

Students are accustomed to multimedia education. You may want to incorporate videos in your classes. However, be careful. Finding good career videos can be difficult. I highly recommend the following.

Down But Not Out: The Inspiring Story of Alphonso Bailey (Indianapolis, IN: JIST Publishing, 2003)

Exploring Your Career Options (Indianapolis, IN: JIST Publishing, 2004)

Real Life 101 series, (Ponte Vedra Beach, FL: Media Pro, 2001)

Resources for Volunteering

Following are just a few different resources to look into to help students get involved in their community. The Web sites link to hundreds of other Web sites and organizations that have opportunities (some are even paid!) for involvement.

Web Sites

www.bmf.net–Black media foundation

www.cme.org/youth/youthcivicculture.html–Center for media education

www.servenet.org–Servenet Web site on service and volunteerism

www.acorn.org–Association of Community Organizations for Reform Now

www.americorps.org–AmeriCorps

www.amnesty.org–Amnesty International

www.citycares.org–City Cares

www.cityyear.org–City Year

www.crossculturalsolutions.org–Cross Cultural Solutions

www.gardenclub.org–National Garden Clubs, Inc.

www.globalservicecorps.org–Global Service Corps (GSC)

www.globalvolunteers.org–Global Volunteers, Partners in Development

www.habitat.org–Habitat for Humanity

www.idealist.org–Idealist and Action Without Borders

www.lionsclubs.org–Lions Club International

www.lookgoodfeelbetter.org–Look Good...Feel Better, For Women in Cancer Treatment

www.mentoring.org–Mentor, National Mentoring Partnership

www.nationalservice.org–Corporation for National and Community Service

www.ncpc.org–National Crime Prevention Council

www.networkforgood.org–Network for Good, Resources for Nonprofit Organizations

www.nwf.org–National Wildlife Federation

www.pointsoflight.org–Points of Light Foundation

www.policevolunteers.org–Volunteers in Police Service (VIPS)

www.publicallies.org–Public Allies

www.redcross.org–The Red Cross

www.rotary.org–Rotary Foundation

www.unitedway.org–United Way

www.USAFreedomCorps.–USA Freedom Corps, a government program

www.VFP.org–Volunteers For Peace

www.volunteer.gov/gov–Volunteer.Gov/Gov, Building America's Communities of Service

www.volunteerinternational.org–An up-to-date search site for international volunteer and internship opportunities

www.volunteermatch.org–Volunteer Match

www.volunteersofamerica.org–Volunteers of America

www.yar.org–Center for Youth as Resources

www.youthactivism.com–Activism 2000 project

www.youthforanimals.org–YCA, Youth Corps for Animals

www.ysa.org–Youth Service America

Books

Ausenda, Fabio, and Erin McLoskey, eds. *World Volunteers: The World Guide to Humanitarian and Development Volunteering.* (Bedfordshire, England: Universe Books, 2003)

Hall, Colin, and Ron Liebier. *Taking Time Off.* (New York: Princeton Review, 2003)

Lewis, Barbara A., and Pamela Espeland. *The Kid's Guide to Service Projects: Over 500 Service Ideas for Young People Who Want to Make a Difference.* (Minneapolis, MN: Free Spirit Publishing, 1995)

Powell, Joan, ed. *Alternatives to the Peace Corps: A Directory of Third World & U.S. Volunteer Opportunities.* (Oakland, CA: Food First Books, 2001)

Resources for Careers

Following are just a few resources that will help students in their career exploration process. Use these, but don't just stop here. There are many more out there.

Web Sites

www.jist.com–JIST Publishing, Inc., a career reference center

http://online.onetcenter.org–Career exploration Web site

www.acinet.org–America's Career Info Network

www.bls.gov/oco–Occupational Outlook Handbook

www.career-lifeskills.com–Career/LifeSkills Resource, Inc.

www.careernetwork.org–Career planning and adult development network www.careers.org–Career resource center

www.careertrainer.com–Career Research and Testing, Inc.

www.dowhatyoulove.com–Practical guide to career change and personal renewal

www.higherawareness.com–Web site to help you get to know and grow yourself

www.jobhuntersbible.com–From author of *What Color Is Your Parachute?*; can take career quizzes on site

www.ncda.org–National Career Development Association

www.PersonalityType.com–The Personality Type Toolkit

www.princetonreview.com/cte/quiz/career_quiz1.asp–Online career quiz from Princeton Review

Books

Farr, Michael. *The World of Work and You: A Self-Directed Guide to Exploring Career and Learning Options.* (Indianapolis, IN: JIST Works, 2002)

Farr, Michael. *Career & Life Explorer.* (Indianapolis, IN: JIST Works, 2002)

Lindsay, Norene. *Dream Catchers: Developing Career and Educational Awareness.* (Indianapolis, IN: JIST Works, 2004)

Lindsay, Norene. *Pathfinder: Exploring Career and Educational Paths.* (Indianapolis, IN: JIST Works, 1999)

Boles, Richard N. *How to Find Your Mission in Life.* (Berkeley, CA: Ten Speed Press, 2001)

Edwards, Lloyd. *Discerning Your Spiritual Gifts.* (Cambridge, MA: Cowley Publications, 1988)

Edwards, Paul and Sarah. *Finding Your Perfect Work: The New Career Guide to Making a Living, Creating a Life.* (New York: J. P. Tarcher, 1996)

Gale, Linda. *Discover What You're Best At.* (New York: Simon & Schuster, 1998)

Griffiths, Bob. *Do What You Love for the Rest of Your Life: A Practical Guide to Career Change and Personal Renewal.* (New York: Ballantine Books, 2001)

Kishel, Gregory and Patricia. *How to Start, Run and Stay in Business.* (New York: John Wiley & Sons, 1998)

Mattson, Ralph T., and Arthur F. Mills. *Finding a Job You Can Love.* (Nashua, NH: P & R Press, 1999)

Moore, Christopher Chamberlin. *What I Really Want to Do....How to Discover the Right Job.* (St. Louis, MO: Chalice Press, 1989)

Orndorff, Robert. *Peterson's The Insider's Guide to Finding the Perfect Job.* (Lawrenceville, NJ: Peterson's, 2000)

Savon, Bret, and Elliot Goldman. *It's Who You Know: How to Make the Right Business Connections—and Make Them Pay Off.* (New York: Berkley Books, 2001)

Sinetar, Marsha. *Do What You Love, the Money Will Follow: Discovering Your Right Livelihood.* (New York: Dell Publishing, 1989)

Taub, Marci, and L. Michelle Tullier. *Work Smart: The 250 Smart Moves Your Boss Already Knows.* (New York: Princeton Review, 1998)

Tullier, Michelle; Tim Haft; Marci Taub; and Meg Heenehan. *The Princeton Review: Job Smart.* (New York: Princeton Review, 1997)

Weiler, Nicolas W., and Stephen C. Schoonover. *Your Soul at Work: Five Steps to a More Fulfilling Career and Life.* (Mahwah, NJ: Hidden Spring, 2001)

Gonna Stay in the Game?

Deciding to Never Stop Learning

Chapter Objectives

- Understand the value of higher education
- Recognize the types of colleges
- Recognize alternatives to college
- Understand financial aid programs
- Apply the information about higher education

Introduction

These sessions introduce students to the importance of college/higher education and open the realm of possibility of going to college. Many of the activities also engage the youth in critical thinking and social justice issues.

While this chapter does discuss a variety of postsecondary options, it is very college/university content heavy. More specifically, it is geared at having the students consider four-year colleges as opposed to junior colleges. Why? Our society values a college degree. I understand that college is not for everyone, but I also know that many people rule out college because they think they will never be able to get in either because of family situations, financial reasons, or due to poor grades. And, from what I have experienced with my work in Chicago, many students are never given college as a realistic option. It seems to be a someday-maybe-far-in-the-future, or yeah-like-*YOU*-could-really-go-to-college option. But if the student has the heart to believe he or she can do it, it is possible. As a single mother paying her way through college, I was told by almost everyone, even the financial assistance officers at the college, that I would never be able to afford going to school with a child. I was told I should either go to a community college or go to school part-time and work full-time so that I could support my family and pay for school. Well, they were wrong. I went to school full-time, graduated with my bachelor's in four years (despite having my second baby two days before graduation), and finished a two-year graduate program in two years. I didn't believe that, just because I made a few bad choices, I should suffer my whole life for them. I wanted my education and I was going to get it, so I did, despite all the negativity almost everyone gave me. It just goes to show that anything is possible if you only believe! And this is the type of attitude that needs to be fostered in these sessions.

Classroom Configurations

The classroom setup varies from session to session. I recommend that the desks are in a circle or semicircle rather than in rows. I generally try to start the classes with a whole-class activity or an activity involving small groups of two or three. Using activities gets the students involved in that day's topic in a hands-on way, engaging their attention right away.

Chapter Outline

Topic I.   Why Should I Keep on Learnin'?

      A.   Know What's Out There

      B.   Role Playing: You're the Career Counselor

      C.   Don't Get Left Behind

Topic II.   Say What? Me Go to College?

      A.   You Make the Decision

B.   The Possibilities Are Endless

C.   Alternative Admissions Programs

Topic III.   What If I Can't Hang with College (Just Yet)

A.   Everyone Has Options

B.   Find Out What's There

Topic IV.   Show Me the Money

A.   The Truth About Money for School

B.   Don't Overlook Scholarships

C.   Just Be Yourself

Topic V.   What's It Take to Get into a School?

A.   Get Organized

B.   Take One Step at a Time

Topic VI.   How Can I Find the Perfect School for Me?

A.   Check Out the School's Expectations

B.   Interview the School

C.   Explore the Campus

Presentation Plan

The following section illustrates my methods of presenting the material to students, incorporating the activities found in the *Your Promising Future* workbook. You will want to adapt the methods and schedule to meet the needs of your students and situation.

Session One

Introduction This session gets students thinking about education, its purpose, and how it can change lives. It will also introduce students to the various types of schools that are out there.

Pretest Hand out a short quiz to test the students' knowledge of the content before the presentation. (See the "Chapter 2 Test" section.)

Icebreaker 1: College Fest Students are challenged to think about the variety of schools available.

Objectives	Recognize the names of institutions of higher education
	Build teamwork skills
Materials	Paper and pencil
Procedure	1. Students form six groups.
	2. Give the students four minutes to come up with as many colleges as they can think of in the area only (i.e., within their city or county).
	3. Give the groups four more minutes to list the colleges in the state.
	4. Give the groups five minutes to list the colleges outside of the state.
	5. At the end of the activity, each group should read their lists to the class. Someone can record the answers on a notepad or chalkboard in front and tally how many (unduplicated) schools the entire class was able to come up with.
	6. You can make this activity a challenge and award a prize to the group that comes up with the longest combined list.
Rules	1. Select a captain for your team, the one who will write down all the answers the group comes up with.
	2. Select a spokesperson to share the responses with the class at the end of the activity.
Time	20 minutes
Notes/Tips	To segue into the class activity, you may want to ask the students how they know about some of the schools. (Some may know them just because of their sports teams or for their fraternities or parties, and so on.) After students respond, ask them how going to college can change their life situations. Then lead them into the "Why Should I Keep On Learnin'?" worksheet.

(continues)

(continued)

Activity: Why Should I Keep On Learnin'? Students can remain in groups they formed for icebreaker. Each group will be given one of the scenarios. Students will discuss the scenario and think of solutions to the problem, answering the questions in the worksheet.

Objectives	Understand the value of higher education
	Build teamwork skills
	Develop critical-thinking skills
	Develop problem-solving skills

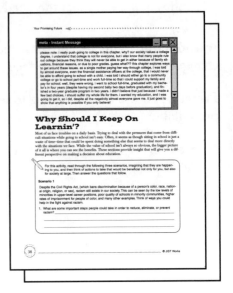

Materials	Scenarios in the workbook or create others that are more relevant to your community, the worksheet, and pencil
Procedure	1. If you don't do the icebreaker, divide the students into groups of four.
	2. Assign a scenario to each group.
	3. Ask the students to discuss the scenario assigned, trying to come to a consensus on how to solve the problem.
	4. Write the answers in the workbook.
	5. Tell students that they have 15 minutes on this before regrouping.
	6. Regroup and discuss.
Time	25 minutes
Notes/Tips	For the discussion, the teacher should read each scenario one at a time. After reading the first scenario, each group that responded to that scenario should be asked to provide their responses. Continue for each scenario.

Following are two more scenarios that you can use that are not in the workbook.

Scenario 1: You live at home with your three brothers, one sister, your mother, and your grandmother who is 72 and in poor health. Your mom works six days a week, 12 hours a day, and still barely brings in enough money to pay the bills and feed the family. At 16, you are the oldest, and your siblings are all under the age of 10. What are some of the ways you can help your mom out? Apply the questions in the workbook to this scenario and find a solution.

Scenario 2: Your little sister has been sick a lot lately, so your mom took her to the doctor for some testing. They got the results back and found out she has cancer. The doctor says her chances of survival are 50/50 and recommends an expensive and time-consuming method of treatment. Your parents work long

Session One

hours and have insurance, but this treatment isn't fully covered. They will still have to pay thousands of dollars for it. What can you do? Apply the questions in the workbook to this scenario and find a solution.

Homework: Know What's Out There The students match the names and descriptions of different types of education.

Objective	Understand the differences among types of schools
Materials	Worksheet and pencil
Procedure	This can be done in class or taken home as homework.

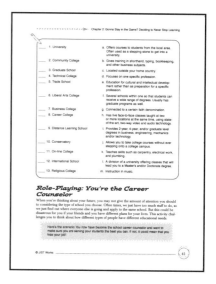

Introduction Students learn about the variation of types of postsecondary educational opportunities. This session focuses on the importance of finding a school that is right for the individual students.

Icebreaker 2: It's Shoe Time Students are challenged to come up with a product that is designed to fit the needs of a specific person.

Objectives	Apply problem-solving skills
	Build teamwork
	Develop communication skills
Materials	Four different types of shoes or pictures of shoes. (You can substitute something other than shoes, but just use objects that are obviously different in size, color, or shape.)
Procedure	1. Place the shoes on a table at the front of the room.
	2. Give each group one of these descriptions:

I'm a runner. I run four miles everyday. I am thinking about training for a marathon, so I'll need to make sure that I get a shoe that will last through the miles.

I love playing ball. Anytime I see a court, I'm there. The only problem is that I twisted my ankle six months ago and I still have problems at times. I need to make sure it is supported. I may end up paying a little more for my shoes, but I need the support.

I get bored easily, so I always do something different in my workouts. This week I went to step aerobics on Monday, kick-boxing on Tuesday, Thursday was yoga (Wednesday a friend and I went power shopping—what a workout that was), and Friday I rode the stationary bike. As a student, I am on a budget, so I need a pair of shoes that will work with anything.

(continues)

Session Two

Session Two

(continued)

I hate exercising. Forget the stairs, give me an elevator. I just need something that looks good. I can't be seen with some ugly-looking shoes. That's not right. I just got this new outfit, these jeans and a red shirt; I need some sneakers that will sport nicely with it.

3. Ask the students to decide which shoe fits the description they have, allowing them to come to the front to examine the articles. The articles must be left on the table; students cannot take them back to their desks.

4. Set a four-minute time limit.

5. At the end of the time, have a representative from each group read the description, tell which shoe they thought was theirs, and give a justification for their findings.

Time   10 minutes

Notes/Tips   To segue into the next activity after the group presentations, ask the students if just any shoe would have worked for their person. The answer should be "no." Then ask, "Why?" Some answers are that it wouldn't be comfortable, would slow them down, might cause injury, and so on.

The same is true of school. People have different needs and learning styles. If they went to just any school and it didn't fit their style, they wouldn't feel right. The discomfort could be very detrimental to their school performance and jade their outlook on their careers or even life. So it's important for students to know what they want and what their options are before looking into school. In the following activity, they learn how to do this.

Role-Playing: You're the Career Counselor Students pretend to be a career counselor giving advice to students.

Objectives   Apply knowledge of types of schools to different students' situations

Recognize that everyone has options

Recognize the talents, abilities, and desires they have and explore their options

Materials   Workbook and pencil

Procedure   1. Assign a student profile to each group.

2. Ask each group to determine which school is best for the student they were assigned.

3. Students discuss the options available.

4. The class reconvenes.

5. One student from each group reports the group's decision to the entire class.

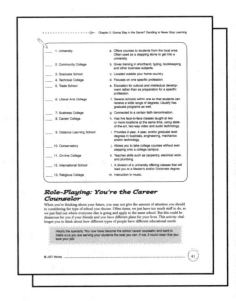

Time   10 minutes for activity, 10 minutes for discussion

Homework: Don't Get Left Behind Students apply the information they've learned thus far to a real person's life.

Objective	Apply knowledge of educational options
Materials	Worksheet and pencil
Procedure	1. Students do this activity independently.
	2. Share their findings with the class.
Notes/Tips	This can be completed in-class if you have extra time or it can be done as homework.

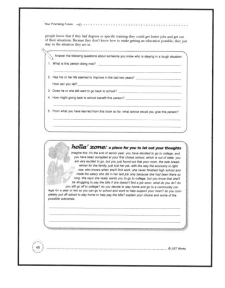

Homework: holla' zone Give students a scenario and ask them to respond in a journal.

Objectives	Apply knowledge of educational options
	Develop critical-thinking skills
Materials	Workbook and pencil
Notes/Tips	This can be a homework assignment. If students want to share holla' zones, you could spend a session doing a wrap-up before beginning the next topic. In this session, you can talk about the holla' zones and integrate some of the activities from the class topics and discussion section.

Introduction This session takes the students through the various options available to them if they choose to go to college.

Icebreaker 3: Same Difference Students learn that the same option doesn't produce the same result for everyone.

Objectives	Develop critical-thinking skills
	Build team work
Materials	Association cards, paper, and pencil
Procedure	1. Students form groups of twos.
	2. Pass out an "association card" to each group.
	3. Go over the rules and give students 10 minutes to complete the activity.
	4. Reconvene as a class and have some of the students share their responses.
	5. Discuss how their responses differed from their partner's response.
Rules	1. Each student should have one piece of paper and a pencil.
	2. When the students get the association card, they should read the word or phrases on it and then, on their own sheets of paper, write a short story about that word or phrase.
	3. Students should not share their responses with their partner until both are finished.

(continues)

Session Three

Session Three

(continued)

4. After both students have finished writing, have them share with each other their responses, noting the similarities and differences between their responses.

Time	15 minutes
Notes/Tips	When you discuss as a class, point out how each word or phrase did not mean the same thing to each person. This is similar to choosing a school. We all have our own interests and styles, so even if our best friend is going to a certain school, that doesn't mean it's the right school for us.

Activity: You Make the Decision The students focus on their educational future.

Objective	Apply information about education to personal life
Materials	Worksheet and pencil
Procedure	1. Ask students to answer the questions on the worksheet alone.
	2. When completed, students should get with their partner to discuss their responses.
	3. The entire class should reconvene and share thoughts on the activity.
Time	25 minutes
Notes/Tips	During discussion, the worksheet does not address the result of people's decision to go or not to go to college. This would be something to highlight in a discussion. Ask the students where some of these people are now; the positive and negative results of the choice they made. What sort of impact does this have on the student's life?

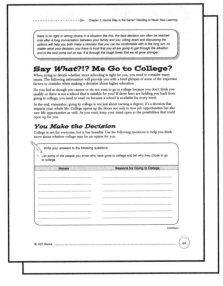

Homework: The Possibilities Are Endless Students explore the factors to consider in selecting a college.

Objective	Apply information about education to personal life
Materials	Worksheet and pencil
Procedure	1. Ask students to read the workbook pages and respond to the questions.
	2. Discuss the students' responses.
Notes/Tips	This worksheet should be done to fill time or as homework. Discussion is optional.

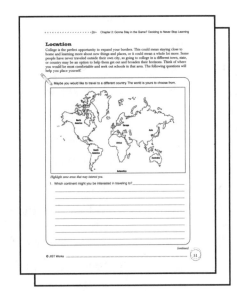

Activity: Alternative Admissions Programs Each student completes a quick checklist of alternative admissions programs.

Objective	Apply information about education to personal life
Materials	Worksheet and pencil
Procedure	1. Ask students to answer the questions on the worksheet.
	2. Discuss the students' responses.
Time	10 minutes
Notes/Tips	This can be done with "The Possibilities Are Endless" worksheet.

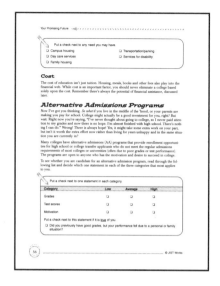

The point of this session is to let kids know that there are many different ways to be able to get into school. They shouldn't let grades stop them from exploring. It also is important to let students know that they have to be knowledgeable about their options and vocal about wanting to go on to college.

Just knowing about available programs helps a student: The person doesn't have to know specifics. Sometimes college counselors won't even mention programs to a student because either the counselors don't know or may not think that the student is very serious about school due to the high school performance. If a student mentions the program, the counselors pick up on the fact that that student has researched the school and isn't just some kid who thinks he or she can go to college to party some more. Being aware shows counselors that the kid is serious and has potential not demonstrated in high school.

Homework: holla' zone Each student writes a description of the ideal college experience.

Objective	Apply information about education to personal life
Materials	Worksheet and pencil
Notes/Tips	This can be done as a homework assignment. If students want to share holla' zones, you could spend a session doing a wrap-up before beginning the next topic. In this session, you could talk about the holla' zones and integrate some of the activities from the "Suggestions and Teaching Tips" section into this session.

Introduction Whether a student goes to college or not, finding a job that pays a decent, livable wage requires some sort of training. This session takes a look at different educational options in various job fields.

Icebreaker 4: Everyone Has Options This timed word search helps students identify alternatives to college.

Objective Identify alternatives to college

Materials Worksheet, pencil, timer, and prize(s)

Procedure

1. Divide the students into groups of two.

2. Make sure that students have pencils and then ask them to open their workbooks to the page <u>before</u> the word search (using the page number, not the words "word search").

3. Announce that the group with the most correct words in the word search within three minutes gets a prize.

4. Tell the students to begin the word search, and turn on the timer at the same time.

5. When the timer goes off, have the groups count the number of found words.

6. Award prizes to the pair that has found the most words.

Time 10 minutes

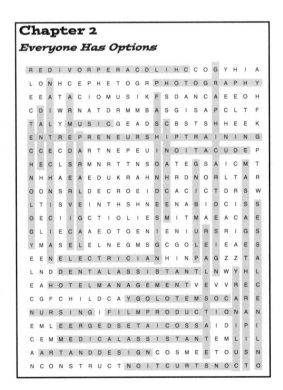

Activity: Find Out What's There Students are challenged to find out more about training required for specific fields.

Objective	Determine the requirements for a specific career or careers
Materials	Worksheet, pencil, Internet, telephone, or the library
Procedure	1. Students complete the worksheet.
	2. Ask several students to share their findings.
Time	35 minutes
Notes/Tips	Make sure to schedule the library or Internet time for this activity.
	You can extend this activity by having students write a report or create a project about what they learned. One thing that the students could do is create a career fair in which they have a poster board–type presentation of their career field, and then some literature about some schools (local and national) that offer training programs.

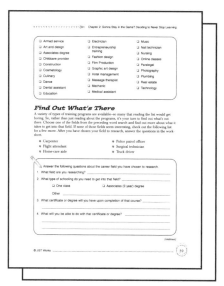

Activity: holla' zone Each student writes an honest assessment of his or her level of commitment to education.

Objective	Apply information about education to personal life
Materials	Worksheet and pencil

Session Five

Introduction This session is designed to break through the financial barriers to going to school.

Material	Script:
	Obviously it costs money to go to school, so you cannot completely ignore the price factor when deciding what college to go to. Fortunately, though, many avenues are available to help you finance your way through school. In this session, we explore those avenues. One means for paying for school is scholarships, the topic of the next icebreaker.

Icebreaker 5: Scholarships Granted Students get a feel for how scholarships are awarded.

Objective	Recognize that getting a scholarship is possible
Materials	Icebreaker questions and prizes
Procedure	1. Pass out worksheet "Scholarships Granted" (in the "Suggestions" section) to students, giving them five minutes to answer the questions.
	2. Tell the students you have a "scholarship" available for the students who meet the criteria (see "Scholarship Criteria" on page 65).

(continues)

Session Five

(continued)

3. Read the first requirement on the sheet and ask those students who meet that requirement to come to the front of the room.

4. Read the next requirement. If this requirement doesn't apply to those who are standing, they should sit down.

5. Continue reading requirements until only one student is remaining. Award the scholarship to this person.

Time 10 minutes

Notes/Tips If you get to a point where more than one student is standing or one question puts the last few people back in their seats, keep these people up and have them come up with a reason that they deserve the "scholarship." Award the prize to the best response (you can even have the other students help you decide this).

Activity: The Truth About Money for School Students learn key facts about financial aid.

Objective Recognize the possibility of financial assistance for postsecondary education

Materials Two groups, prizes, and the worksheet

Procedure

1. Divide the class into two teams.

2. Appoint a person to keep score.

3. Read the questions and have the teams guess whether the answer is true or false.

4. If the answer is false, allow the group a bonus point if the members know the correct response.

5. Discuss the activity as a class.

Time 15 minutes

Notes/Tips Because the answers are located in the books, you have to watch that the students do not look at the answers first. It may be best to tell the students to put away their workbooks until after this game. This way, even if they have looked at the answers, they may not remember them. If you find that many students have looked at the answers, you may want to start just a general discussion and ask the students what their original thought was for the answer and why. Any way you do this activity, it is important to go over how this session applies to the students.

One area that I have had to really highlight is the information about wards of the state. I've encountered many students who are wards of the state or in some capacity of being "independent." These students generally have many options available to them to help pay for college. If they have a case worker, the case worker should know about some sort of college-bound program that they can get into. Regardless of any program through the child welfare system, though, the FAFSA would show that they have an expected family contribution of $0 and would totally qualify for financial assistance. Most of the money would come in terms of grants, money they don't have to pay back. This is very important for them to know.

Additionally, students should know that the money they get for school can also be used to help pay for living expenses, such as an apartment—if they don't live on campus. Most often, students get refund checks (all in one lump sum, so the kids have to learn to budget the money) that can support them through the semester. They shouldn't have to work so much, if at all.

Activity: Just Be Yourself Students pretend to be applying for a focus group.

Objective	Understand what facts about themselves will be requested when applying for scholarships
Materials	Worksheet and pencil
Procedure	1. Students complete the worksheet.
	2. Ask a few students to share their worksheet answers.
Time	10 minutes
Notes/Tips	A point to make to the students in this activity is that this person was willing to go all out to get these tickets, something that most kids can relate to. When they feel as though something is important to them, they will come up with the money or whatever needs to be done. They should have the same attitude about college. Some

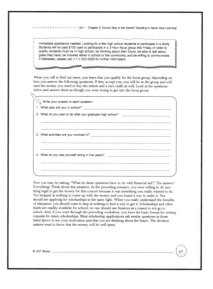

people will look at the focus group and think, "I don't really have an interest in this sort of thing, but I can get the money I need, so I'll just go on and do it." Shift that focus to school. A student may not want to go to school, but if it's what is going to provide him or her with the desired job, income, house, travel opportunities, and all the other things, they'll think it's worth it.

Activity: Practice Makes Perfect: Request for a Scholarship
Students write a letter, requesting a scholarship.

Objective	Apply knowledge of how to apply for a scholarship
Materials	Worksheet and pencil
Procedure	1. Ask students to turn to the information they supplied in the "Just Be Yourself" worksheet.
	2. Ask them to write a letter, requesting a scholarship.

(continues)

Session Five

(continued)

3. Students then exchange their letters with classmates.

4. Ask students to proofread and evaluate the effectiveness of their classmates' letters.

Time   10 minutes

Notes/Tips   When the students write their letters, it is important that they demonstrate a passion. The only way to get noticed is to have their letter stand out among all the rest.

Activity: holla' zone This holla' zone should be done at home. Students discuss it at the next class, if desired.

Materials   Worksheet and pencil

Time   10 minutes

Session Six

Introduction Going to college is not like going to high school. There are many different aspects students have to look at to decide which is the right school for them. Also, the application process doesn't happen right before school starts. This session gives the students a better understanding of the college planning process.

Icebreaker 6: Peanut Butter and School Planning Sandwich A student volunteers to make a peanut butter–and-jelly sandwich.

Objective   Understand that activities in life follow established steps or processes.

Materials   Peanut butter, jelly, knife, bread, plate, paper, and pencil for writing instructions

Procedure   1. Set out the materials on the table.

2. Ask students to write instructions for making a PB&J sandwich with only the materials on the table.

3. Ask students to turn in their instructions.

4. Instruct a student volunteer to make the sandwich, using only the instructions on the paper. Tell him or her not to do anything unless it's written on the paper.

Time   10 minutes

Notes/Tips   Most students will forget to write instructions such as "open jar." Instead they will write "Put peanut butter on bread." The student volunteer should put the peanut butter jar on the bread. As the student begins to follow the directions on making a sandwich, it will become apparent that the little details about making the sandwich are very important to the process.

To relate this to college planning, a student can't just think, "I want to go to college" and then wait until August when school starts to just go and register for school. There are many steps in applying for college or any postsecondary educational opportunity, especially if you want to get financial support. Thus, it is important to start early and find out all the steps.

Activity: Get Organized Groups of students decide where to insert college-preparatory tasks into a planning calendar.

Objectives	Understand the steps to applying to colleges
	Develop teamwork skills
	Develop a personal college application timeline
Materials	Four sets of cards containing the steps to submitting a college application, four game boards, a flip chart showing the steps to submitting a college application, a planning calendar, worksheets, and prizes

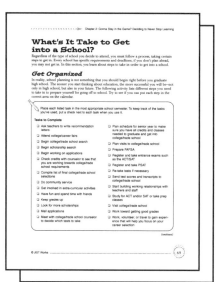

Procedure	1. Write each step necessary for the college planning calendar on a strip of paper. Make four complete sets.
	2. Divide the students into four groups.
	3. Hand each group a game board and a set of the steps.
	4. Give students 10 minutes to put each step into the correct spot on the calendar.
	5. Award prizes to the group that either gets all the steps in the correct spot or is the closest to getting them all right.
	6. Ask students to transfer the information to their personal planning calendar page in the workbook.
Time	15 minutes
Notes/Tip	Ideal prizes would be either a planner or some small book about college. Even if the student doesn't use it, he or she can give it to someone who can, or it still plants a seed about using these resources.

Activity: Take One Step at a Time Students assess where they are in the planning process and what they need to do.

Objective	Apply the information about the college application process to personal situation
Materials	Workbook and pencil
Procedure	1. Ask students to evaluate where they are in the process by answering the questions on the workbook page.
	2. Ask several students to share their answers.

(continues)

Session Six

(continued)

3. Discuss the questions and the students' answers.

Time — 20 minutes

Notes/Tips — It would be a good idea to get a college counselor either from the school or some nearby college/university to talk about the college planning process.

Activity: holla' zone Students respond on an emotional level to the information on the process for applying to college.

Objective — Evaluate personal attitudes toward the process for applying to college

Materials — Worksheet and pencil

Time — 10 minutes

Session Seven

Introduction Deciding on the right school can be difficult. Students won't know whether a school will be a good match just by reading its brochures or talking to friends. Brochures and friends are biased and tell only a portion of the story. To get the information they need to determine whether the school is right for them, as they do when looking for a job, they must ask questions and check it out in person. You need to schedule some Internet time for this session.

Icebreaker 7: Getting to Know You Students get into groups of two and find out about their partner's interests in a school.

Objectives — Develop communication skills

Practice interviewing skills

Materials — Pencil, paper, and a partner

Procedure —
1. Students get into groups of two.

2. Pass out questions (in "Suggestions" section) for students to ask.

3. Students write down their partner's response.

4. Ask a few students to share responses.

Time — 10 minutes

Notes/Tips — This activity not only gives students new perspectives on their peers, but also gets each person thinking about some of the requirements they have of a school.

Activity: Check Out the School's Expectations Students record information about themselves that they'll need to supply on an application for college.

Objective	Gather information for college applications
Materials	Worksheet and pencil
Procedure	1. Ask students to complete worksheet.
	2. Remind them that this information will help guide them in the next two activities.
Time	10 minutes

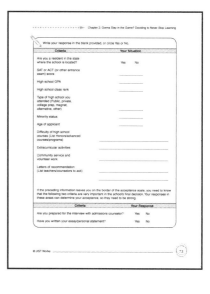

Activity/Homework: Interview the School Each student gathers information about a school.

Objectives	Gather specific information about the school
	Develop communication skills
Materials	Worksheet and pencil
Procedure	1. Ask each student to select a school that is interesting to him or her.
	2. During class, students should look on the Internet for information about the school that interests them.
	3. They should answer as many questions on the worksheet as they can from what they find, but also think of other questions that may come up while searching.
	4. They should also be looking for information that will address the next worksheet ("Explore the Campus") as well.
	5. For homework, instruct the students to contact the school they researched and gather the information requested on the worksheet.
Time	20 minutes
Notes/Tips	Because college exploration is probably a new thing for most of these students, it is best to discuss a bit what college offers. Stress that because college offers so much and everyone has different needs, it is best that students do a lot of exploration and asking questions.
	It may be a good idea to talk about some of your experiences and questions you had when you began your college search. If you can think of any "embarrassing moments" to provide, this can be helpful to show students that we all have to learn somehow, and it's okay to ask, no matter how trivial you think the question is.

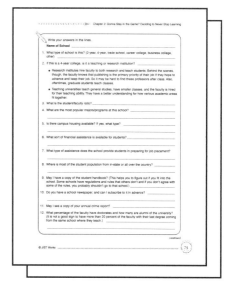

(continues)

(continued)

One example I like to use from my past (and you are welcome to use this and credit me for it) is when my older sister began college searching. I went with her to some schools out in California. At USC (University of Southern California, a very prestigious school), we were talking about dorm life. The college counselor began talking about meal plans and said the university offered something like a 10-meal plan, 5-meal plan, and 3-meal plan. And my question to him was, "A DAY?" My eyes were wide, and there was a huge smile across my face at the thought of having that many meals a day, but to my disappointment, he meant a week. From there on out though, I knew what counselors meant when they were talking about meal plans.

Activity: Explore the Campus Take a field trip to a local college or tech school to show the students how to conduct themselves and what to look for on a campus visit.

Objectives	Record information about the school
	Understand how to conduct site visits and make evaluations
Materials	Workbook, pencil, and field trip forms
Procedure	1. Take a field trip to a college or university in the area.
	2. Instruct the students to answer the questions in the workbook as though they were considering attending this school.
	3. Discuss the questions in the workbook.
Time	Potentially one session
Notes/Tips	You should encourage the students to go out on their own and explore some colleges that they are interested in attending.

Activity: holla' zone Students respond to the information they gathered about the school.

Objective	Evaluate the decision he or she made regarding a school
Materials	Worksheet and pencil
Time	10 minutes

Video The section about education and training in *Explorig Your Career Options* reinforces the key concepts in this chapter.

Posttest Hand out a short quiz to test the students' knowledge of the content after the presentation. (See the "Chapter 2 Test" section.)

Materials	Form and pencil
Time	10 minutes

Feedback Using the template in the back of this guide, create a feedback form that gives the students an opportunity to react emotionally and intellectually to the information presented in this chapter.

Materials	Form and pencil
Time	10 minutes

Suggestions and Teaching Tips

It is very important to address critical-thinking skills used in this chapter, especially in the holla' zone sections. The activities throughout the book require these skills. If they aren't fostered from the beginning, it will be difficult to keep the students engaged.

Icebreakers

Following are elements you need for the icebreakers presented in this chapter.

Icebreaker 3: Association Cards

For this icebreaker, you can either print the form and then cut it into sections or, using index-type cards, write one of the following words or phrases. Make enough cards for the entire class when it is divided into groups of two. You can also come up with some of your own.

Sports	Money	Raise a child
Harlem	Business	Heal the sick
Farmers	Factories	Solve problems
The world	Downtown	Answer the phones
Growing up	Dancing	Winning the gold
Chicago	Los Angeles	Finishing the race
Gangs	Develop	Getting out
Airplanes	Learn	Never give up
The flag	Build a home	Singing

Icebreaker 5: Scholarships Granted

Take a look at the following categories and list as many of your characteristics as you can think of in each category.

Racial and ethnic background

Do you know your family tree? What different racial and ethnic backgrounds do you have? (Many people have backgrounds they didn't know about.)

Family status and background

Write down the following information:

What is/are your parent's job(s)?

Are you the first generation in your family to go to college?

Are you an immigrant who became a U.S. citizen?

Are you the first generation in the U.S.?

What is your country of origin?

What is your family income or status?

Do your family members belong to any civic or community organizations?

Are your parents alumni of any particular college or university?

Personal characteristics

What are your personal characteristics? Some might include being a single parent; paying your way through school; or special skills, talents, or interests.

Physical characteristics

What are your physical characteristics? Here are some examples: Left-handed, two different colored eyes (naturally), a disability, or hair color.

Activities

What activities are you involved in? Think of any sports, music, volunteer/community service, clubs, activism, babysitting, work, and community organizations you may be involved in.

Field of study

What field(s) are you considering going into?

Scholarship Criteria

Tell the students that you have one scholarship to award (and make sure you have a prize to offer them. I try to avoid candy as I am highly health conscious. I would give something like a small gift certificate.) In this icebreaker, the students are to act as though they are all planning to go to college, and they are all looking for scholarships. Tell the students that if the criteria fits them, they should come to the front of the room for the first one only. After that, if it doesn't apply to them, they need to sit back down. Use the following criteria to qualify students for the scholarship.

1. Racial/ethnic background. For this, choose the most dominant background in the class. You want to start with as many students as possible for this activity.

2. Family background: This scholarship is for those who would be first generation going to college. (All students are supposed to pretend as though they are going to college, so don't have them sit down just because they say they don't want to go to college.)

3. Areas of interest: The student who will receive this scholarship should have an interest in the arts, whether it is music, theater, film, or visual art.

4. Physical characteristic: This scholarship is for left-handed people. The student must demonstrate ability to write with his or her left hand.

5. The student must have at least two (cumulative) months of volunteer experience in any area.

6. Field of study: The student must be interested in pursuing a career in either business or design.

If more than one student remains, find other characteristics to single one out or have the students give a two-minute speech on why they would like the scholarship (related to their future goals).

Icebreaker 7: Getting to Know You

Hand out one copy of these questions to the students:

1. If you went away to school, would you like to live in dorms, off campus, or in a fraternity or sorority house?

2. What opportunities would you like to be offered if you went to college?

3. What is the most interesting aspect of college? (I.e., regardless of whether you plan to attend college or not, what draws you the most to going to college?)

4. What type of college would you be most interested in attending?

Class Topics and Discussions

If you have a few free minutes or if you're having trouble engaging the students or you know of particular situations in the lives of the students that could benefit from discussion, you may want to initiate a discussion of any or all of these topics:

- Have a career fair as a part of this chapter, inviting representatives from local colleges and schools to speak to the group for 10-15 minutes, with time for students to meet with them individually after all the guests speak.

- Have the students be responsible for the college fair. Each student could select a school, conduct research, and make a presentation to the entire group.

- Ask an alumnus from the students' school to speak about his or her experiences at college.

- Obtain the FAFSA CD from the government and play it for the students.

- Get a state map for each student, and ask them to locate all the colleges, universities, and trade schools in the state.

- Ask a group of speakers, either from the community or who had to overcome some obstacles to go to college, to talk about their lives and the benefits of education.

- Invite some older students from an alternative school, who had dropped out of high school and are now trying to complete school, and have them talk about why they left school, what brought them back to school, and where they see their futures going because of school. If you do use this suggestion, you really have to make sure you bring in students who have positive outlooks to school and are not doing it because they are made to, either by some legal mandate or other reason. For the session to be most successful, they have to be doing this because they see a value in school.

PowerPoint Slides

I have prepared several PowerPoint slides to accompany this chapter and present them here as pages that you can copy to hand out, convert to transparencies, or scan to create PowerPoint presentations. However, if you would like to have the actual PowerPoint slides, please contact your JIST representative at 1-800-648-5478 or check out our Web site at www.jist.com.

The ACT

- **What:** Tests your educational development and college competence in math, reading, science, and English.

- **Grading System:** Highest possible score is 36. (Can be converted to an SAT score.)

- **Who Accepts the Test:** Widely used in the Midwestern states, but accepted by most U.S. universities and colleges.

- **When to Take:** Spring of your junior year or early senior year so you can retake if you want to improve your scores.

The SAT

- **What:** Tests academic level. Used as an admission standard. (Additional SAT II subject tests show more about your academic level but are not required by all schools.)

- **Grading System:** Highest possible score is 1600—800 on math and 800 on verbal. (Can convert this score to an approximate ACT score.)

- **Who Accepts the Test:** Most universities on the East and West coasts.

- **When to Take:** Spring of junior year or early in senior year so you can retake if you want to improve your scores.

Other Entrance Exams

- **ABLE:** Adult Basic Learning Examination
- **ACT ASSET:** ACT Assessment of Skills for Successful Entry and Transfer
- **CAT:** California Achievement Test
- **PAA:** Prueba de Aptitude Academica (Spanish-language version of the SAT)
- **PSAT:** Preliminary SAT
- **SCAT:** Scholastic College Aptitude Test
- **TABE:** Test of Adult Basic Education
- **TOEFL:** Test of English as a Foreign Language (for international students whose native language is not English)

Pre-Junior Year

- Get involved in extracurricular activities
- Start building working relationships with teachers and staff
- Work toward getting good grades

Fall Junior Year

- Check credits with counselor to see that you are working toward college requirements
- Begin college search
- Register and take PSAT
- Keep grades up
- Do community service
- Study for ACT and/or SAT, taking prep classes if necessary

Spring Junior Year

- Meet with college counselor to decide which tests to take
- Plan schedule for senior year to make sure you have all credits and classes needed to graduate and get into college
- Attend college fairs
- Register and take college entrance exams—ACT/SAT

Summer Before Senior Year

- Plan visits to colleges
- Work, volunteer, or travel to gain experience that will help you focus on your college selection
- Begin working on college applications

Fall Senior Year

- Visit colleges
- Begin scholarship search
- Ask teachers to write recommendation letters
- Compile list of final college selections
- Mail applications
- Re-take tests if necessary
- Send test scores and transcripts to colleges

Spring Senior Year

- Prepare FAFSA
- Look for more scholarships
- Have fun and spend time with friends
- Finish strong

Outside Class Activities and Homework

What do you do if you know that your message isn't getting through to one of your students? Why don't you try a different approach? In this section, I offer a few suggestions that focus on the visual, auditory, and kinesthetic learning styles. Let my suggestions just be a starting point for you, though. Use your imagination, creativity, and knowledge of your students to come up with even more effective methods of communicating the message.

TOPICS	LEARNING STYLES		
	Visual	**Auditory**	**Kinesthetic**
Need for Further Education	Prepare a poster or collage illustrating the different living conditions of the educated and uneducated.	Create a recording of small children enjoying learning or an older person reflecting back on the role of education in his/her life.	Create a mime act, illustrating the principle that having an education opens doors for people.
Types of Schools	Write a play or script about the different types of schools.	Put together a soundtrack to accompany the play that classmates wrote.	Act out the play that classmates wrote.
Schools Student Might Want to Attend	Collect brochures for schools and make a collage or poster.	Record an interview with an admissions representative or student from the school you want to attend.	Build a model of the campus of a school you'd like to attend.
Sources of Financial Aid	Write a letter to a politician to complain about recent cuts in financial aid for students attending colleges.	The government will send out a CD explaining the FAFSA to anyone (and cassettes to visually impaired) FREE. Auditory learners can phone and request one at 1-800-4-FED-AID. They then can give a short report on what they learned from the recording.	Visit at least five schools and make a collection of their financial aid brochures.

Chapter 2 Test

I always give a pretest as a way of introducing students to the upcoming topics and discovering what they already know. I do not discuss the answers on the pretest. I then administer the same test as a posttest, discussing the answers within the same class period.

In Appendix B, you will find additional questions you may want to use, depending upon the requirements for the sessions that you're teaching.

Name _____

Date _____

Chapter 2 College Planning

Circle the letter of the best answer.

1. When is the best time to start investigating colleges?

    a. The summer before starting college

    b. The end of sophomore year

    c. The end of junior year

    d. The middle of junior year

    e. The middle of senior year

2. Ideally, one should take the ACT:

    a. Spring junior year

    b. Fall junior year

    c. Fall senior year

    d. Spring senior year

    e. Never

3. The FAFSA is

    a. a test needed to get into college.

    b. the federal form that determines one's financial need for college.

    c. a type of grant that students can get to help pay for college.

    d. None of the above

4. What is *not* a way people can pay for college?

    a. Work

    b. Take out loans

    c. Get scholarships

    d. Write school off on their tax returns

    e. Play a sport

5. Your grades in school are average, but your test scores are low. You really want to go to College X, but you don't know if you'll be accepted. It is the middle of senior year so there is only so much you can do to improve. What should you *not* do?

    a. Accept the fact that you just won't be able to go to school.

    b. You could attend a community college for a year or two, show that you are determined to make it, and then apply to College X.

    c. Look to see if College X has an alternative admissions policy that might allow you in under special conditions.

    d. All of the above

6. What are some of the reasons why some people delay going to college?

    a. They need a break from rigors of going to school.

    b. They have no real idea of the purpose in going to college.

    c. They don't have the funds.

    d. They have a particular family situation that makes it hard to go to college.

    e. All of the above

Chapter 2 College Planning Answers

1. b
2. a
3. b
4. d
5. a
6. e

Resources

Following are Web sites and books that you may find helpful. Remember that Web site addresses frequently change. If a site is no longer active, try using a search engine to locate the organization's current Web site.

Resources for College

The following are just some of the resources out there to help students in their college search.

Web Sites

www.campustours.com–Campus Tours: Virtual college campus tours

www.collegeboard.org–The College Board, a national nonprofit membership organization providing information about colleges

www.collegeispossible.org–College Is Possible

www.ed.gov–U.S. Department of Education

www.nacac.com/fairs.html–National Association for College Admission Counseling

www.testprep.com–Information about SAT and other prep tests

Books

Fogg, Neeta P.; Paul E. Harrington; and Thomas F. Harrington. *The College Majors Handbook.* (Indianapolis, IN: JIST Publishing, 1999)

Gordon, Rachel Singer, and Anne Wolfinger. *Best Career and Education Web Sites.* (Indianapolis, IN: JIST Publishing, 2004)

Greenfeld, Barbara C., and Robert A. Weinstein. *The Kids' College Almanac.* (Indianapolis, IN: JIST Publishing, 2000)

Bauld, Harry. *On Writing the College Application Essay.* (New York: HarperResource, 1987)

Linamen, Larry Ed.D. *Guide for the College Bound: Everything You Need to Know.* (Grand Rapids, MI: Fleming H. Revell, 1998)

Lockerbie, D. Bruce, and Donald R. Fonseca. *College: Getting In and Staying In* (Grand Rapids, MI: Wm. B Eerdmann Publishing, 1990)

Mangrum, Charles T. *Peterson's Colleges with Programs for Students with Learning Disabilities or Attention Deficit Disorders.* (Princeton, NJ: Peterson's, 2000). Available from JIST Publishing.

Nemko, Marty. *You're Gonna Love This College Guide.* (Hauppauge, NY: Barrons Educational Series, Inc., 1999)

Peterson's. *Peterson's Guide to Four-Year Colleges.* (Princeton, NJ: Peterson's, 2003). Available from JIST Publishing.

Resources for Noncollege Options

If college isn't an option, here are some resources that students can search or read for other educational programs that will help them succeed in life.

Web Sites

www.jist.com–JIST Publishing, Inc., a career reference center

www.overview.com–An overview of trade schools, vocational schools, and more

www.rwm.org–RWM vocational school database

www.technical-trade-schools.com–Technical Trade Schools, a directory of online and on-campus vocational and trade schools nationwide

Books

Broadway Books. *Success Without College* series. (New York: Broadway Books, 2001). Available from JIST Publishing.

Ferguson Publishing. *150 Great Tech Prep Careers.* (Chicago, IL: Ferguson Publishing Company, 2001). Available from JIST Publishing.

Oakes, Elizabeth (Ed.). *Guide to Apprenticeship Programs.* (Chicago, IL: Ferguson Publishing Company, 1998). Available from JIST Publishing.

Peterson's. *Peterson's Internships 2004.* (Lawrenceville, NJ: Peterson's, 2003). Available from JIST Publishing.

Peterson's. *Peterson's Guide to Two-Year Colleges.* (Lawrenceville, NJ: Peterson's, 2003). Available from JIST Publishing.

Phifer, Paul. *Great Careers in 2 Years: The Associate Degree Option.* (Chicago, IL: Ferguson Publishing Company, 2003). Available from JIST Publishing.

The Rosen Publishing Group, *Cool Careers without College* series. (New York: The Rosen Publishing Group)

Resources for Financial Aid

You may find these resources helpful for students wanting to find money for school.

Web Sites

http://scholarships.salliemae.com–Funding for higher education

www.BlackExcel.org–Black Excel, the College Help Network

www.collegenet.com–CollegeNet, helping students complete applications for admission

www.college-scholarships.com–Easy access to information about scholarships

www.ed.gov–U.S. Department of Education

www.fastweb.com–FastWeb, finding money for college

www.finaid.org–FinAid, student's guide to financial aid

Books

Clark, Andy; Karen Breslow; and Amy Clark (Eds.). *Athletic Scholarships: Thousands of Grants– And Over $400 Million–For College-Bound Athletes.* (New York: Facts on File, 2000)

Diers, Rochelle; Mary L. Hershberger Thun; and Susan R. Treinen. *How to Buy a College Education: A Consumer Planning Guide Featuring RealCosts, RealMoney, RealChoices.* (Minneapolis, MN: The Access Group, Inc., 1996)

Hastings, Penny, and Todd D. Caven. *How to Win a Sports Scholarship.* (First Base Sports, Inc., 1999)

Kaplan. *Kaplan Scholarships 2003.* (New York: Kaplan, 2002)

Kaplan, Benjamin R. *How to Go to College Almost for Free.* (New York: HarperCollins, 2001)

Lesko, Matthew, and Mary Ann Martello. *Free College and Training Money for Women.* (Omaha, NE: infoUSA, Inc., 2000)

Mazzoni, Wayne. *The Athletic Recruiting & Scholarship Guide.* (Bridgeport, CT: Mazz Marketing, 1998)

McKee, Cynthia Ruiz. *Cash for College.* (New York: Quill, 1999)

Peterson's. *Peterson's Scholarship Almanac 2004.* (Lawrenceville, NJ: Peterson's, 2003). Available from JIST Publishing.

Peterson's. *Scholarships, Grants & Prizes 2004.* (Lawrenceville, NJ: Peterson's, 2003). Available from JIST Publishing.

Sourcebooks Trade. *The Minority and Women's Complete Scholarship Book.* (Napierville, IL: Sourcebooks Trade, 1998)

Wheeler, Dion. *A Parent's and Student Athlete's Guide to Athletic Scholarships: Getting Money Without Being Taken for a (Full) Ride.* (New York: McGraw-Hill/Contemporary Books, 2000)

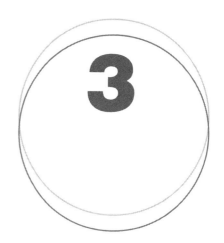

Got Skillz for Your Game?

Developing Skills for Success

Chapter Objectives

- Understand the role of patience in becoming successful
- Apply teamwork skills learned in previous chapters
- Integrate knowledge of educational and career paths with personal goal-setting
- Recognize the characteristics required of leaders

Introduction

The sessions in this chapter are designed to help students gain character traits that are essential in almost any job. These sessions are crucial as employers note that these are traits many high school and college graduates lack today.

Classroom Configurations

The classroom setup varies from session to session. I recommend that the desks are in a circle or semicircle rather than in rows. I generally try to start the classes with a whole-class activity or an activity involving small groups of two or three. Using activities gets the students involved in that day's topic in a hands-on way, engaging their attention right away.

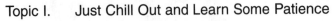

Chapter Outline

Topic I.   Just Chill Out and Learn Some Patience

      A. Choose Your Own Adventure

      B. Wait for the Best

Topic II.   Teamwork: How Work Gets Done

      A. Team Up: Two Heads Are Better Than One

      B. Teamwork Builds Better Business

      C. Role-Playing: A New Business Venture

Topic III.   Goals That Get You to the Top

      A. The Lowdown on Goal Setting

      B. Goals for Life

      C. Practice Makes Perfect: Taking It Step by Step

      D. Let Your Goals Be Your Guide

Topic IV.   Leadership: Do You Have What It Takes?

      A. Become a Leader

B. Let's Get to Work

C. Speak Up!

Presentation Schedule

The following section illustrates my methods of presenting the material to students, incorporating the activities found in the *Your Promising Future* workbook. You will want to adapt the methods and schedule to meet the needs of your students and situation.

Session One

Introduction At the beginning of the book, we talked about having to sacrifice some things in order to reach our dreams. This session helps to develop those skills in the students.

| Notes/Tips | This session uses the terms *patience* and *delayed gratification* interchangeably. |
| Pretest | Hand out a short quiz to test the students' pre-chapter knowledge. (See the "Chapter 3 Test" section.) |

Icebreaker 1: Thank-You Cards Students make two thank-you cards.

Objectives	Understand the concept of delayed gratification
	Apply the concept of delayed gratification
Materials	Construction paper, scissors, paint, glue sticks, beads, buttons, craft items, and envelopes
Procedure	1. Put all materials needed to make thank-you cards on a table in the front of the room.
	2. Write rules for the thank-you cards on the board.
	3. Instruct students that they will have eight minutes to make two thank-you cards.
	4. On the first card, have the students write "Thank you" on the front and, on the inside, "For the interview. I'll take the job." They should decorate the front of the second card but leave the interior blank.
	5. When students finish the first card, they should immediately put the card (which should still be damp from gluing) into an envelope and seal it. They should leave the second card out on the desk until further directions.
	6. Have the students pass the sealed cards to the person next to them.

7. Have the person receiving the thank-you note open it. Ask all the students, "If an employer received this card, would she or he want to hire the person who sent it? Why not?"

8. Generate a five-minute discussion on the preceding questions. See tips below to help.

9. After discussion, have students open up the second card and write some benefits to waiting and learning more before taking on a new project.

10. Have the students put the second note in an envelope and pass it to the person beside of them. (Do not tell the students this will be done until after they have finished writing the benefits of waiting).

11. Instruct the students receiving the second thank-you note to open it, and ask the class about the difference that waiting a few minutes made. Let students share their responses with the class.

Rules	1. Require that the students use objects that take time to dry, but the objects must be dry before the end of the class time. 2. Ask that the students save a little room on the front for writing and leave the inside of the cards blank until you tell them what to write.
Time	20 minutes
Notes/Tips	This session is to help students learn the skill of delayed gratification. The first card that the students made is like someone who is trying to rush into something they are not ready for. As the card was going into the envelope, it probably looked really nice and could have impressed anyone, but it was sent before it was dry, so it was ruined. This is what happens to people. In the job arena, we want to be able to be the boss or be doing what it is that we want to do for our life right now, but if we go in too early, we'll probably get confused and overwhelmed—smeared like the card. Remind the students that it is not that they're not smart or not a good worker or anything like that; it is just that they need to learn some things before they can get to exactly where they want to go. We can all be anything we want to be, but there is a process we need to go through, some steps we need to learn, before we can get to the top. Several students have asked: "Why do I have to work at a retail store? Why can't I just start out owning my own business?" Well, in order to run a business, you have to know what it takes to run a business. Working different jobs and going to school helps one learn the many different facets about owning a business.

Activity: Choose Your Own Adventure This scenario-based worksheet illustrates the point that the quickest route may seem like the best way to get where you want to be in life, but the quickest way often leaves us with less than we expected.

Objective	Apply the principle of delayed gratification to three different scenarios
Materials	Worksheet and pencil
Procedure	1. Have the students get into groups of three. 2. Before working as a group, each student reads through each scenario and makes a decision.

(continues)

Session One

(continued)

3. Before going on to the answer section, the students share their choices and discuss with the other members why they made that decision.

4. Students should then read the workbook pages that give the results.

5. Ask students to share what they learned during this activity.

Time 20 minutes

Notes/Tips An effective way to end this activity is to have students give examples of delayed gratification from their own or others' lives.

List some of the benefits to waiting (more prepared, more appreciative of what you get, better opportunities). Ask students to brainstorm for even more benefits.

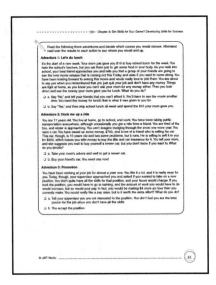

Session Two

Introduction Students continue to work on developing patience, or delayed gratification. This time they will apply their knowledge to the education arena.

Icebreaker 2: Sweet Rewards Students gain tangible result for being patient.

Objective Recognize the value of patience

Materials Candy

Procedure 1. Before beginning, go over the two "rules" with the students.

2. Hand out a piece of candy to each student.

3. Begin "Wait for the Best" activity right away.

4. Stop the class 15 minutes before the end and pass out more candy to those who waited.

Rules 1. Everybody receives a piece of candy.

2. They can eat candy right away, but if they wait until the end of class before eating it, they can get another piece of candy.

Time 2 minutes at beginning, 15 minutes at end of class

Notes/Tips At the end of the class, ask the students why they were willing to wait for the candy. Was it difficult to wait? Why or why not? How were they able to put the desire to eat the candy behind them so that they could wait? Were they distracted by the candy? How did they overcome this distraction? How can they apply this lesson to life?

Activity: Wait for the Best This activity presents students with a scenario and asks them to make a decision about the best course of action.

Objectives	Interpret a chart
	Apply principle of delayed gratification to a situation
	Judge which is the best of two options
	Apply teamwork skills
Materials	PowerPoint slide, worksheet, and pencil
Procedure	1. Divide students into several small groups.

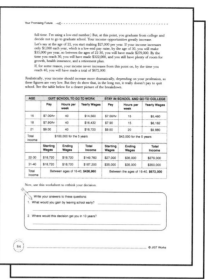

2. Before opening their workbooks, put up the "Wait for the Best" slide (see PowerPoint section) and ask one student to read the bulleted items.

3. Give the groups three minutes to discuss the scenario and decide what they would advise the student to do and why.

4. Have each group select a representative who then shares which option they selected and why.

5. Have the students open their workbooks to the activity.

6. Put up the chart "Cost of Quitting" and discuss the impact of education on earning potential.

7. Have students answer the questions in their groups.

8. Have each group select a new representative who then shares the group's response.

Time	25 minutes
Notes/Tips	This activity shows the long-term benefits of an education. It is important to note that the salaries for those who dropped out of school are higher-end salaries, and the salaries for staying in school are low-end salaries. The actual benefit of going to school is much higher than the chart shows. There are many other benefits from going to college that are not reflected in a salary. Some of these benefits are networking, name recognition, ability to be in certain professional groups, and so on.

Have the students discuss the pros and cons to each side. It's easy to say "stay in school," but that can be difficult to hear when there is no food on the table.

Question for discussion: What arguments can you give for delayed gratification in these situations?

Remember: Stop this activity 15 minutes before the end of class so you can distribute the candy used in the icebreaker. Try to integrate the icebreaker discussion with this discussion.

(continues)

Session Two

(continued)

Homework: holla' zone Students react on a personal level to the principle of delayed gratification

Objectives	Apply principle to personal life
	Recognize failures to delay gratification
	Develop a personal plan to strengthen ability to delay gratification
Materials	Worksheet and pencil
Notes/Tips	This should be done at home, but students can begin it in class if there is extra time.

Session Three

Introduction Students work on developing teamwork skills.

Icebreaker 3: Build a Team Groups of students work together to build a project.

Objectives	Understand the role of teamwork
	Apply teamwork skills
Materials	Legos or other building materials to create a project
Procedure	1. Divide students into three groups and give each group a set of Legos or other material for the project.
	2. Tell the students that they have five minutes to build the tallest structure possible.
	3. At the end of five minutes, ask students to judge which building is the largest.
	4. Discuss the role of teamwork in achieving the best structure.
Rules	1. Students should work together (i.e., no one should be on the side doing something else).
	2. Students can share materials with other groups if desired.
Time	10 minutes
Notes/Tips	At the end of five minutes, compare the building sizes and then ask if they've really made the biggest building that they could have made. They will probably say yes because each group has used all the blocks it had, but, unless the whole class worked together (which was not originally instructed) the answer is no. The instructions never said the groups could not have worked together. If all groups put their blocks together they could have made the biggest building.
	In the world of work, we are given projects that need to be completed in a specific timeframe. Often, we do not have all the tools we need to accomplish that project on our own, or at the best quality. The best way to accomplish the task then is working with others. This is often a problem in the workplace because many people want to take all the credit or are unwilling to share ideas. The results from teamwork are often much more effective and efficient in the long run. Nowadays, companies are looking for employees who know how to work on a team and share ideas and responsibilities.

Activity: Team Up! Students brainstorm on solutions to an assigned problem, illustrating TEAM (Together Everyone Achieves More).

Objectives	Understand the benefit of teamwork
	Apply the principle of teamwork
	Strengthen teamwork skills
Materials	Worksheet and pencil
Procedure	1. Divide students into groups of three and give each group an assigned project.
	2. Ask this question: Who needs to be on the team if this project is to be successfully completed?
	3. Tell the students that they have five minutes to come up with possibilities.
	4. After five minutes of working on their project, ask the groups to tally the number of jobs they wrote, write that number down on the top of their paper, and draw a star next to it. Then have two students from each group switch groups, each person going to a different group (that is, if one group originally consists of Tom, Jo, and Sam, Tom and Sam should leave. The people leaving should go to groups that have different projects. Jo should get two new partners from two different groups, and Tom and Sam should not join the same new group).
	5. Give the new groups five minutes to come up with more jobs.
	6. After the second group has met, ask students to tally the number of jobs added to the list, put that number at the top of the paper, and draw a circle next to it. Were they able to come up with any new ideas?
	7. Share the results.
Time	20 minutes
Notes/Tips	Each group needs to come up with the different types of assistance they would need in order to accomplish the project. For example: If the group project is to build a house, the project team needs to include architects, carpenters, electricians, plumbers, cabinetmakers, bricklayers, and so on. The students need to come up with these and other types of workers who could help build a house.

Introduction Students continue working on building teamwork skills.

Icebreaker 4: Building Structures Students use communication and teamwork skills to formulate a word.

Objectives	Recognize the role of effective communication in teamwork
	Understand the value of sharing ideas
Materials	Index cards with letters on them
Procedure	1. Hand each student an index card with a letter on it.
	2. Explain that the objective of this game is to come up with the longest word possible using each person's letter only once.
	3. Students will then mingle with other students to try to come up with a word. Explain that there will be more than one word formed, so don't try to use all the letters in one word. Divide into groups and come up with a word.
	4. After 10 minutes, stop the class and see how many words were formulated and which group has the longest word.
	5. Award prizes.
Rules	1. Students can be in only one group.
	2. You must work together to come up with the longest word possible. The word does not have to be in English, but if it is in another language, the students have to have the correct spelling and know what it means.
Time	15 minutes
Notes/Tips	When making the index cards, make sure to do multiples of vowels and common letters such as s, d, t, l, m, n, c, h, r, and w.
	To make a transition into the next activity, the following information might help:
	On your index card, you had one letter. For some people, this could have actually formed a word, such as I or a, but for most, your letter wasn't very productive until it joined with other letters. In life, we all have skills, talents, and abilities that can be utilized alone, but often more can be done when we combine our talents with others. The only way we know how to combine those talents is if we can communicate and be creative, brainstorming new ways to work together.

Activity: Role-Playing: A New Business Venture Students use a scenario to come up with a new program for a company using the skills already in-house.

Objectives	Recognize various skills and talents
	Integrate skills and talents to create new projects
Materials	Worksheet and pencil
Procedure	1. Form groups of five.
	2. Read over the scenario as a group.

3. Have groups come up with a new project for company described in scenario using the staff. Use the questions following the descriptions to guide them.

4. Give students 15 minutes to complete this activity. If some groups are done quickly, have them come up with another project.

5. Share with class the project ideas each group came up with.

Time	25 minutes
Notes/Tips	Students can get very creative about this activity. There are many different types of projects that this company could embark on. If students are having difficulty figuring out what to write about, challenge the students to think about their lives and communities and what is needed. Then have them find skills or talents of the people described that can help to fill that need.

Activity: holla' zone Students list the negative and positive aspects of teamwork and write about their personal experiences with working as a team.

Objectives	Understand the benefit of working as a team
	Apply the knowledge of working as a team to personal experiences
	Judge whether situations in the personal life can benefit from working as a team
Materials	Worksheet and pencil
Notes/Tips	The holla' zone can be used as a filler if there is extra time in class.

Introduction Students continue to work on team-building skills as they also work on setting goals.

Icebreaker 5: Puzzled? Set a Goal First Students plan how to complete a small jigsaw puzzle and then document and evaluate their plan.

Objectives	Understand the importance of goal setting
	Apply goal setting techniques to a project
	Judge whether having a plan helped
	Use critical-thinking skills
Materials	Several small jigsaw puzzles of 20 or so pieces, paper, and pencil
Procedure	1. Divide the students into groups of four.
	2. Ask each group to select a leader.
	3. Give each group one of the puzzles.

Session Five

(continues)

(continued)

4. Before opening the box, ask the group to discuss the steps they will take to complete the puzzle, with the leader writing down the steps they plan to take. Give them 4 minutes to do this.

5. After the leaders finish writing the planned steps, the groups work the puzzles and the leader records the steps that they actually took. (Give no more than 10 minutes to complete the puzzle.)

6. Each group then discusses the plan and the actual process.

7. At the end, have the groups share with the class how well they followed their planned goal in completing the process. What were some things that came up for the groups as they were doing this?

Rules	Students must work together to finish the puzzle. One person should not be left to complete this alone.
Time	20 minutes
Notes/Tips	To relate the icebreaker to the activity, here is a suggested text:

Often when we look at different aspects of who we are, they are like puzzle pieces. Each aspect has its own form and part to our lives, but until they are combined, they do not represent us. In order to put those pieces together though, we have to have some goals and visions to see how they can all come together and make us who we want to become.

Activity: Goals for Life Students work as a class to come up with different goals for seven "life" areas.

Objective	Recognize ways to set goals for all areas of life
Materials	Marker, big flip chart, worksheet, and pencil
Procedure	1. Have the seven different life arenas listed on a big sheet of paper.
	2. As a group, go over each section and have the students call out as many goals as they can think of that people would set for each area.
	3. Have the students pick a few on their own goals and write them down in their workbook. (If they want to come up with some that weren't mentioned in the class, they are welcome to do that as well.)
	4. Discuss some of the reasons people set these goals.
Time	20 minutes
Notes/Tips	This activity, if done as a group, helps students brainstorm the many goals that could be set. Often youth set goals, but if their minds aren't open to a myriad of possibilities, their goals will be limited. This will help draw out new ideas in the students, and help you, the instructor, see where their level of

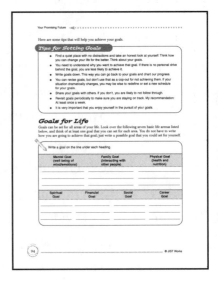

thinking is. It may be necessary for you to help generate some goals outside of what they are used to in order to challenge them. Even if you think that no student would set some of the goals you suggest, just dropping those seeds may spark something in students and grow into something wonderful.

Activity: Practice Makes Perfect: Taking It Step by Step Students work on personal immediate, short-term, and long-term goals.

Objectives	Know the different types of goals
	Apply goal-setting knowledge to personal life
Materials	Worksheet and pencil
Procedure	1. Ask students to complete the worksheet on goal setting.
	2. Make yourself available to answer questions.
	3. Students should be encouraged to share their goals with the class.
Time	15 minutes
Notes/Tips	Begin this activity after the group discussion from Goals for Life. Students need to finish the activity at home and have it ready to complete the next session.
	As the activity asks them to set one goal for one week from that day, I would suggest asking a few students if they would like to be held accountable for a goal and report the following week on the status of that goal, whether they accomplished it, and the result.

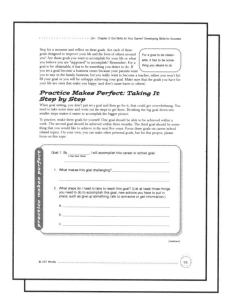

Introduction Students continue working on goal setting.

Icebreaker 6: The End Result Students come up with a product that results from each scenario.

Objective	Understand the importance of breaking a challenging goal into smaller steps
Materials	End Result scenarios and prizes
Procedure	1. Students form groups of four.
	2. The instructor reads the scenarios (see the PowerPoint slides).
	3. When a group knows the answer, the members can raise their hands and call it out.
	4. If the answer is wrong, continue. If the answer is correct, go on to next scenario.
	5. Award prizes for each scenario.

(continues)

Session Six

(continued)

Time	15 minutes
Notes/Tips	As you read each scenario to the students, read one step at a time. If you have the steps on a screen for the students to read, cover up all steps unless you have read or are reading it. Allow the students the opportunity to answer after each step.

To segue into the day's activity, here is a suggested script:

> For this activity, you saw how each step led to a specific result. In and of themselves, the steps may not have seemed as though they were productive, but in the end, something great was achieved. Setting goals is the same. Each step is a small part, but if we keep the big picture in mind, we have something to look forward to and the payoff is great.

> For the cookies scenario, for example, someone wouldn't just pull out any ingredients and throw them together and wait to see what they had. They would probably think: I want some cookies. Then they would have to go through the process of making them, which isn't always fun, but if the person keeps in mind that at the end they will have a great treat, they will complete the steps it takes to make the cookies.

Activity: Let Your Goals Be Your Guide Students focus on their goals and make them meaningful for their lives.

Objective	Understand the value of setting goals
Materials	Worksheet and pencil
Procedure	1. Divide the class into groups of two and appoint each student to be Student A or Student B.
	2. Student B asks the questions on the worksheet to Student A.
	3. Student A shares his or her responses with Student B.
	4. Student B helps to either refine goals or gives new insights to Student A.
	5. Give seven minutes for this.
	6. After seven minutes, have Student A ask Student B the questions.
	7. After seven minutes, have all the groups stop and then discuss the activity as a class.
Time	20 minutes
Notes/Tips	Following are questions you may want to ask the students during discussion:

> Did this activity help you make more meaningful goals? How?

> Did your partner have good insight? What are some suggestions?

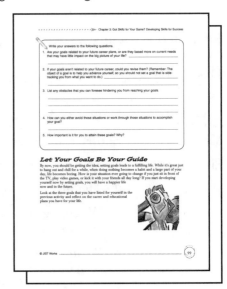

What are some things that the partner noticed about your interest in the goals?

Did this activity help you learn more about yourself? How?

Activity: holla' zone Students evaluate personal goals and set plans for achieving them.

Objectives	Understand the benefit of setting goals
	Apply the knowledge of how to set goals to personal goals
	Judge the effectiveness of the goals
Materials	Worksheet and pencil

Video Chapter point "It's Time to Begin" in *Exploring Your Career Options* fits nicely here.

Session Seven

Introduction Students look at new ways of developing leadership skills.

Icebreaker 7: Let's Get to Work Students complete the worksheet and then use the information on it to complete the activity for the day.

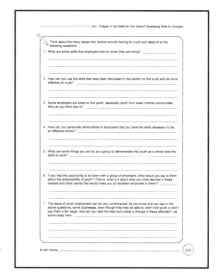

Objective	Apply knowledge of skills involved in leadership to the workplace
Materials	Worksheet and pencil
Procedure	1. Divide students into four groups.
	2. Ask the students to complete the worksheet.
	3. After they've completed the worksheet, discuss their conclusions as a class.
	4. Students remain in these groups and go on to the next worksheet.
Time	10 minutes

Activity: Speak Up! Students complete the worksheet and write a skit to perform or they create a visual project and explain it.

Objectives	Recognize a specific problem or what people perceive as a problem in their community
	Create something that communicates their views on the problem
Materials	Worksheet, lined and unlined paper, video camera, and markers
Procedure	1. Have students remain in groups of four.
	2. Complete the worksheet in the workbook.
	3. Ask students to create something that demonstrates the skills of the members in their group in such a way that they convince employers to hire them.

(continues)

(continued)

Possible projects are a trial of youth versus employers, a news report, a marketing piece for youth employment, or a rap performance.

4. At the next session, ask the students to perform or explain their project.

Time	30 minutes (possible to extend over two sessions)
Notes/Tips	If the skits or projects are excellent, encourage the students to do more with them, such as using them to help market this program to employers, other youth, or social program directors or boards. Obviously this would be a commitment that goes beyond the classroom, but it would be an excellent addition to a resume and a boost for the program.

Homework: Become a Leader Students complete the worksheet individually.

Objectives	Identify current leadership skills
	Identify weaknesses in leadership skills
	Recognize ways to improve leadership skills
Materials	Worksheet and pencil
Procedure	1. Ask students to complete the worksheet.
	2. Give them an opportunity to share their responses.
Time	25 minutes
Notes/Tips	This activity can be completed after "Let's Get to Work" and "Speak Up!", either as a filler for time in class or as homework. If you choose, the students can share their responses.

Homework: holla' zone Students respond individually to the call to leadership.

Objectives	Apply the information learned about leadership to personal lives
	Judge the effectiveness of the effort to be a leader
Materials	Worksheet and pencil

Suggestions and Teaching Tips

In this chapter, it is very important to challenge the students to "think outside the box." The scenarios throughout this chapter introduce ideas and concepts that many of the youth may not be very familiar with. Hence, it may be a bit difficult generating responses. Work with the students and just continue to ask them questions and be prepared to come up with examples yourself.

Class Topics and Discussions

If you have a few free minutes or if you're having trouble engaging the students or you know of particular situations in the lives of the students that could benefit from discussion, you may want to initiate a discussion of any or all of these topics:

- Share stories that illustrate the principle of delayed gratification—both when someone demonstrated it and when someone didn't.
- Have a spoken-word slam. Invite community poets/spoken-word artists to perform on various topics that affect the students' lives (or have the students put together their own jam).
- Take a field trip to some sort of team-building place (such as a field house where a sports team hosts businesses to train them in team-building). Have the students participate in a teamwork day.
- Have the class create some sort of class project, using a goal that they want to see the class as a whole accomplish. It could be some kind of a performance at the school or a community service project, for example.

PowerPoint Slides

We have prepared several PowerPoint slides to accompany this chapter and present them here as pages that you can copy to hand out, convert to transparencies, or scan to create PowerPoint presentations. However, if you would like to have the actual PowerPoint slides, please contact your JIST representative at 1-800-648-5478 or check out our Web site at www.jist.com.

Wait for the Best

The Facts

- 16 years old
- Sophomore in high school
- Lives with mom and brother
- No money for CDs, clothes, or eating out

Wait for the Best

An Option?

Quit school and get a job

Question: Is that a good idea?

Wait for the Best
The Cost of Quitting

Age	Quit school to go to work				Stay in school and go to college			
	Pay	Hours per Week	Yearly Wages		Pay	Hours per Week	Yearly Wages	
16	$7.00/hr	40	$14,560		$7.00/hr	15	$5,460	
18	$7.90/hr	40	$16,432		$7.90/hr	15	$6,162	
21	$9.00/hr	40	$18,720		$9.50/hr	20	$9,880	
Total Income	$100,000 for the 5 years				$43,000 for the 5 years			
	Starting Wages	Ending Wages	Total Income		Starting Wages	Ending Wages	Total Income	
22–30	$18,720	$18,720	$149,760		$27,000	$35,000	$279,000	
31–40	$18,720	$18,720	$187,200		$35,000	$35,000	$350,000	
Total Income	Between the ages of 16–40, $436,960				Between the ages of 16–40, $672,000			

The End Result
Scenario 1

1. Preheat oven to 375°.
2. Mix items in a bowl.
3. Drop spoonfuls onto a baking sheet.
4. Bake until light brown.

What do you have?

The End Result
Scenario 2

1. Watch the weather report.
2. Get sunscreen and a towel.
3. Put food and water in a cooler.
4. Grab keys and sunglasses.

Where are you going?

The End Result
Scenario 3

1. Stretch and warm up.
2. Train a few times a week.
3. Get in line when told.
4. At the sound of the horn, GO!

What are you doing?

Outside Class Activities and Homework

What do you do if you know that your message isn't getting through to one of your students? Why don't you try a different approach? In this section, I offer a few suggestions that focus on the visual, auditory, and kinesthetic learning styles. Let my suggestions just be a starting point for you, though. Use your imagination, creativity, and knowledge of your students to come up with even more effective methods of communicating the message.

TOPICS	LEARNING STYLES		
	Visual	**Auditory**	**Kinesthetic**
Delayed Gratification	Draw a picture or write a story about something from nature that took time to develop.	Make a collection of songs that encourage people to wait or hold on.	Build a model of something that took time to build (a castle, for example).
Teamwork	Think of a new game that requires a group of people to work together, and write out the instructions on how to play the game.	Find a piece of music that requires a group of musicians to work together to produce the sound and explain how each part contributes to the whole.	Think of a new game that requires a group of people to work together and show the class how to play the game.
Leadership	Make a scrapbook of five works by famous artists or designers and make captions, explaining how they affected others.	Put together a CD or tape of speeches or songs and record a sentence or two that explains how each demonstrated leadership.	Make a scrapbook of photos of inventors or sports heroes and write a caption for each photo explaining how the people affected others' lives.

Chapter 3 Test

I always give a pretest as a way of introducing students to the upcoming topics and discovering what they already know. I do not discuss the answers on the pretest. I then administer the same test as a posttest, discussing the answers within the same class period.

In Appendix B, you will find additional questions you may want to use, depending upon the requirements for the sessions that you're teaching.

Name _____

Date _____

Chapter 3 Life Skills

Read the following multiple-choice questions and circle the letter of the best answer.

1. Which of the following is not a skill that all employers seek?

    a. Timeliness

    b. Communication skills

    c. Teamwork

    d. Someone who knows everything

    e. Enthusiasm

    f. Honesty

    g. Flexibility

    h. None of the above

2. What are ways people can get work experience?

    a. Volunteer

    b. Internships

    c. Work

    d. All of the above

    e. None of the above

3. In today's society, what skill do employers say that many recent high school and college graduates lack?

    a. Teamwork and cooperation skills

    b. Communication and specific skill sets

    c. Interview and phone skills

    d. Leadership and integrity skills

4. What are some benefits of teamwork?

    a. You are in an environment that involves frequent change.

    b. You can work with others to come up with new ideas.

    c. You get the job done faster.

    d. You get more vacation time.

    e. More ideas are generated than would be if only one person did the job.

    f. b, c, and e

    g. a, c, and e

Use complete sentences to answer the following two questions.

5. What hesitations might employers have about hiring youth? _____

    _____

    _____

6. Why should an employer hire you? _____

    _____

    _____

Chapter 3 Life Skills Answers

1. d

2. d

3. a

4. f

5. Answers will vary

6. Answers will vary

Resources

Following are some Web sites and books that you may find helpful. Remember that Web site addresses frequently change. If a site is no longer active, try using a search engine to locate the organization that sponsored the inactive site.

Web Sites

www.charactered.net–Character Education Network, a place for students, teachers, schools, and communities to facilitate character education

http://www.globalethics.org/–An organization that promotes ethical behavior in individuals, organizations, and nations

www.yar.org–Youth As Resources, young people from all walks of life taking the lead in community change

www.youthleadership.com–Youth Leadership Development Information Clearinghouse

Books

Bachel, Beverly K. *What Do You Really Want? How to Set a Goal and Go for It! A Guide for Teens.* (Minneapolis, MN: Free Spirit Publishing, 2001)

Blair, Gary Ryan. *Goal Setting 101: How to Set and Achieve a Goal!* (Syracuse, NY: The GoalsGuy, 2000)

Covey, Sean. *The 7 Habits of Highly Effective Teens.* (New York: Fireside, 1998)

McGraw, Jay. *Life Strategies for Teens.* (New York: Fireside, 2000)

Where's the Best Game?

Finding the Job You Want

Chapter Objectives

- Identify personal skills
- Recognize three methods of searching for jobs
- Integrate networking skills into personal life
- Know how to complete an application
- Understand proper phone etiquette

Introduction

These sessions are designed to demonstrate job search techniques. Students will go through several processes to learn how to find a job on their own.

Classroom Configurations

The classroom setup varies from session to session. I recommend that the desks are in a circle or semicircle rather than in rows. I generally try to start the classes with a whole-class activity or an activity involving small groups of two or three. Using activities gets the students involved in that day's topic, engaging their attention right away.

Chapter Outline

Topic I.   Stop Wandering

        A.   Tap into Your Resources by Identifying Your Skills

        B.   Take Stock of What You Have to Offer an Employer

        C.   Understand What Employers Want

        D.   Get Smart

        E.   Don't Rush into Just Any Job!

Topic II.   The Job Board: Use Classified Ads and the Internet to Find Work

        A.   Help Wanted: Check the Paper

B.   Role-Playing: Follow the Classified Ad

C.   Searching the Web: The Wide World of Work

D.   Role-Playing: WWW.JobSeeker.Com

Topic III.   Traditional Job Search Methods Just Don't Cut It Anymore

A.   Networks Aren't Gifts: They're Built

B.   Building Networks

C.   Practice Makes Perfect: Nothing But Net(working)

Topic IV.   Filling Out the Paperwork

        A.   Bad Apps Culd Cost You

        B.   True or False: Completing Applications Takes Practice

        C.   Practice Makes Perfect: Fill Out an Application Please

Topic V.   Can You Talk the Talk?: Phone Etiquette for the Job Search

        A.   Role-Playing: Conducting Phone Interviews

        B.   Answer Business Calls with Class

Presentation Plan

The following section illustrates my methods of presenting the material to students, incorporating the activities found in the *Your Promising Future* workbook. You will want to adapt the methods and schedule to meet the needs of your students and situation.

Session One

Introduction This session helps students identify skills they have that are necessary when looking for a job.

Notes/Tips | Many youth are worried about finding a job because they may not have all the skills they need. Time and again, I have heard youth complain, "I can't find a job because I don't have the experience, but I don't understand how I can get experience without getting a job first." The reality is that they do have skills—even if they have never worked. They just don't know how to identify them. This session helps them learn not only the skills they have that make them marketable, but also the skills that employers look for in employees.

Pretest Hand out a short quiz to test the students' knowledge of the content before the presentation. (See the "Chapter 4 Test" section.)

Icebreaker 1: Sweet Skills Students identify their skills in different areas that correspond to the color of the M&M's candy.

Objective | Identify skills in a sweet manner

Materials | Bowl, M&M's, color chart, pencil, and paper

Procedure |
1. Students take a handful of M&M's. Do not tell them the object of the game. The kids who end up taking a lot will be sorry in the end. The game teaches them not to be greedy.
2. Place the color chart on the board with just the color names written on it.
3. Add the categories to the color names on the color chart.
4. Referencing the color chart, students write down a skill they have for each piece of candy.
5. Students get into groups of four and share their responses with the other members.

Rules | No eating the candy until the instructor gives permission.

Time | 15 minutes

Notes/Tips | You can use other types of candy or objects for this activity. Just be sure to make an appropriate color chart. Because I am very nutrition conscious, I don't like to bring candy into the room, but it was the only thing I could think of that wasn't too costly. Please amend and pass on any other suggestions, as I would love to take out the candy for this activity.

(continues)

(continued)

You have to make a color chart for this icebreaker or write on the board. At the top of the poster board or paper, print "Color Chart." Then list these colors: brown, yellow, red, green, blue, and orange. (I like to use matching marker colors in writing the name of the color.) After the students take the candy, add these categories to the color chart:

Red: Sports they have played

Green: Jobs they have had

Brown: Household chores they have done

Yellow: Things they do after school

Blue: Activities they have done to help other people

Orange: Talents they have

Activity: Tap into Your Resources by Identifying Your Skills Students list skills gained from a variety of activities.

Objectives	Analyze activities to determine skills they require
	Recognize personal life skills
Materials	Worksheet and pencil
Procedure	1. Each student completes the worksheet.
	2. Ask two or three students to share what they learned about themselves by completing the worksheet.
Time	10 minutes

Activity: Take Stock of What You Offer an Employer Students transfer the assessment of their life skills to skills they can use on the job.

Objective	Integrate their awareness of life skills with employment skills
Materials	Worksheet and pencil
Procedure	1. Students complete the worksheet.
	2. Ask students to choose a partner and exchange the previous worksheet and this one with their partner.
	3. Partners read through both worksheets to see whether they overlooked any skills.
	4. Ask students to share what they learned about themselves by completing the worksheets.
Time	25 minutes
Notes/Tips	Students should complete this worksheet, have a brief discussion, and then complete the next one.

It is important to challenge the students to think about activities they have done in the past and extract skills that they used from them. When you lead a class discussion, ask students for what types of activities they wrote about and the skills used. Then help them come up with more ideas. You could even have one student offer to read what he or she wrote and then ask the class to list other skills used for those activities. This should really be done before going on to the next worksheet.

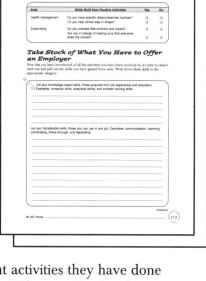

Homework: Understand What Employers Want Students complete the worksheet to determine whether they have the skills that employers are seeking.

Objective	Identify personal strengths and areas that need work
Materials	Worksheet and pencil
Procedure	1. Students complete the worksheet on their own.
	2. Ask a few students to share any insights they had by completing the worksheet.
Notes/Tips	This can be done as either a filler if you have extra time or as homework.

Activity: holla' zone Students think about how to gain skills they currently lack.

Objective	Generate ideas of how they can improve upon their skills
Materials	Worksheet and pencil

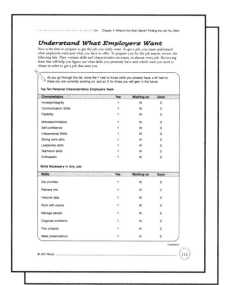

Introduction Students practice using the classified ads to find jobs.

Notes/Tips   There are many different ways to find a job, but if students don't know where to start, a job search can be overwhelming. This session teaches students how to use classified ads to locate jobs for which they are qualified.

Icebreaker 2: Name That Job Students complete a handout and then discuss their answers.

Objective   Recognize sources for jobs

Materials   Worksheet and pencil

Procedure
1. Divide students into groups of four.

2. Give the groups four minutes to answer the following questions:

   Name all the places of employment that you can think of that are within four blocks of school.

   Name all the places of employment within one mile of school.

   List five places you would like to work (they do not have to be in the community).

3. Each group tallies up the number of jobs they have.

4. Ask students to call out the jobs they listed.

5. Write these jobs on a flip chart.

6. Ask whether students want to work at these jobs for the rest of their lives.

7. Point out that they need to be able to search for jobs, not just settle for ones they currently know.

Time   10 minutes

Notes/Tips   When students complete this activity, encourage them to really look through the newspaper to see what all it provides. Students often stop after finding one item that may work for them, but there are many different aspects to the classified ads. Some ads are for schooling, some for job fairs, some for jobs that make them think they can make a lot of money quickly, and so on. Point out all these aspects as you work through this section.

Before going into the next activity, review the tips for using the classified ads (found in their workbooks, "Help Wanted: Check the Paper").

Activity: Role-Playing: Check Out the Classified Ads Small groups of students read four classified ads and answer questions about them.

Objectives	Know what classified ads are
	Interpret information given in classified ads
Materials	Worksheet and pencil
Procedure	1. Divide students into groups of two or three.
	2. Ask them to complete the worksheet together.
	3. When everyone is finished, ask one group to share their answers.
	4. Discuss other possible answers.
Time	15 minutes

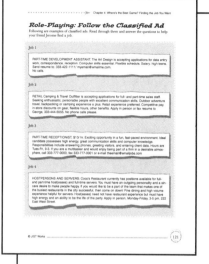

Notes/Tips — Before going into this activity, in the workbook are some tips for using the classified ads. Review those tips.

Additionally, it may help to bring in some newspapers and have the students review them so they have a better understanding of how to use the newspaper in searching for a job.

One technique I have used is to review the newspaper before class and find an ad. I generally try to look for something the students are qualified for because this gets them looking into the correct section. When I find an ad, I create a description of what I am looking for in a job so that it matches the job requirements.

During class, I then tell the students what I am looking for and ask them to find at least one ad that I could apply for. (This is similar to the role-playing done below, but it is specific to the classified ads.)

Session Three

Introduction Students practice using the Internet to find jobs.

Notes/Tips — The Internet isn't always the most efficient way to find a job, as it provides access to millions of people. It is nice, though, as it provides a greater field of job openings, so if students are looking at finding a job away from home, it will be easier.

Icebreaker 3: Web Jobs Students find Internet sites that post jobs.

Objective	Understand how to search the Internet for jobs
Materials	Paper and pencil
Procedure	1. Students form groups of three.
	2. Give the class three minutes to come up with as many Web sites as they can think of to search for jobs on.

(continues)

(continued)

3. Students tally up the lists.

4. Groups read their responses.

5. Record their responses on a flip chart.

Time   10 minutes

Notes/Tips   Before going on to the activity, make sure to go over the tips in the workbook.

Activity: Role-Playing: WWW.JobSeeker.Com Students read the role-playing scenario and find an appropriate job.

Objectives   Know how to use the Internet

Apply information learned on the Internet to a specific job

Materials   Internet access, worksheet, and pencil

Procedure

1. Pre-identify one Web site that you will use and have the students log on.

2. The students read the role-playing scenario and then navigate to job search Web sites.

3. The students then answer the questions on the role-playing worksheet.

4. Discuss their findings and then encourage them to search the Web for jobs that interest them.

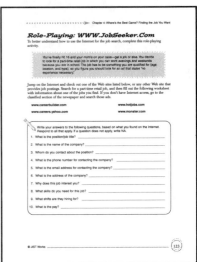

Time   20 minutes

Notes/Tips   Although the workbook lists several Web sites, from experience I find that, when working with a group, it is best to pick one and have the whole class use that site. This way, if there are questions, you can pinpoint the problem and share how to overcome it with the whole class. When I have had students pick a Web site, I have found that everyone starts having problems and asking questions and it becomes difficult to get to all the students.

Activity: holla' zone Students evaluate the role of their first job in gaining skills for their career.

Objective   Understand the transferability of skills

Materials   Worksheet and pencil

Procedure

1. Ask students to reflect back on or think ahead to their first job.

2. Ask them to identify the skills that job provided or will provide and to write a paragraph describing those skills.

Session Four

Introduction Students learn about the value of networking not only in the job search arena, but also in life.

Icebreaker 4: Building Webs The instructor gives a visual demonstration of the ways that we human beings are interconnected.

Objective	Recognize that people rely on each other for help
Materials	Ball of yarn
Procedure	1. The class stands and forms a circle. (This may call for moving the desks).
	2. Start with a ball of yarn in your hands.
	3. Say one thing about yourself that is likely to be something someone else in the room has in common with you.
	4. Ask those who share that trait to raise their hands.
	5. Choose one student, hold onto one end of the yarn, and pass the yarn to the student you chose.
	6. The student receiving the yarn then says something different about himself or herself.
	7. Students raise their hands if they share that trait.
	8. The student holds onto the yarn and passes the rest to the person he or she chose.
	9. The process continues until everyone is holding onto the yarn.
	10. At the end, talk about the ways that knowing others can help us find a job.
Time	15 minutes
Notes/Tips	It is important to point out that all students may not have something in common with every person in the room, but they have something in common with at least one person and that person is connected to at least one other person. These connections can be very helpful when we are in need of something–even a job. It is good for them to know that, by turning to people they know for help, they can connect with possibly hundreds of other people who can help.

Lecture Share the PowerPoint presentation about the ineffectiveness of resumes or present the information on a flip chart.

Objectives	Define networking
	Understand the effectiveness of networking as compared to other methods of job searches
Procedure	1. Ask the students for the most effective way to get a job. (They'll probably suggest that a resume is the most effective way.)

(continues)

(continued)

2. Present these statistics:

Effectiveness of Traditional Job Search Method

- Studies show that an average of 245 resumes are received for every interview granted.

- Four of every five job openings aren't even advertised.

- Many times, though, these unadvertised positions are filled faster than those that are advertised.

3. Show these definitions of networking:

- Network: any systems of lines that cross; a group of people who work together informally to promote common goals.

- Networking: the promotion of political goals or the exchange of ideas and information among people who share interests or causes.

4. Relate an example of a time when someone used the traditional methods of applying for a job and another person used networking and got the job much more quickly.

5. Share the Two-Foot Rule:

Tell anyone and everyone within two feet of you what you need and you will eventually find what you've been looking for.

6. Emphasize the point of the Two-Foot Rule by sharing this: In the job hunt case, when you network, you don't only ask people you think could give you a job, because that limits you and often ends up going nowhere. You tell *everyone* that you are looking for a job and ask whether they know of any openings or if they know where you can go to find further assistance. Oftentimes people may not be able to give you a job personally, but they may know someone who could or a business that is hiring. Or, even if they don't know when you ask, if they hear of something, they may remember you and come back to tell you.

Time   10 minutes

Activity: Building Networks Students are assigned a need and then must contact three people for help with the solution. (You can also have the students select a need from the list on the worksheet.)

Objective   Apply the principle of networking to a specific need

Materials   Worksheet and pencil

Procedure	1. Assign each person a different need.
	2. The students put a check mark by their need and then go around the room, asking people—students and teachers—whether they know how to get help with the need. (They don't actually get the item they need; they just try to come up with a way of possibly obtaining it.)
	3. Students should record their findings on the worksheet.
Time	20 minutes
Notes/Tips	Example: If you need to find a T-shirt from Louisiana, you network and find out that a class-mate's grandma lives in Louisiana and can send one to you.

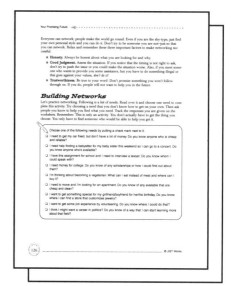

Homework: Practice Makes Perfect: Nothing but Net(working) Students apply what they learned about networking to a real need in their lives.

Objective	Apply principle of networking
Materials	Worksheet and pencil
Procedure	1. The students write the need they're seeking to meet in the bubble.
	2. Tell them to ask people for help in meeting that need, writing the names on the lines stemming from the bubble.
	3. The students should stop asking only when the need is met.
Time	This should be done outside of class, so there is no time limit.

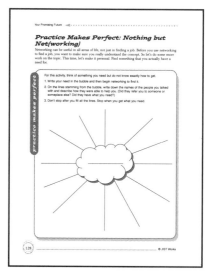

Activity: holla' zone Students develop a statement of what they have to offer an employer. They can then use the statements when requesting networking assistance.

Objective	Integrate the principles of networking with the recognition of personal skills
Materials	Worksheet and pencil

Video Use the chapter point "Networking" in *Exploring Your Career Options* to connect network-ing to the career exploration process.

Introduction Students learn how to complete an application for employment.

Icebreaker 5: Bad Apps Culd Cost You Students see the wrong way to complete an application.

Objective	Identify problems with the way an application has been completed
Materials	Worksheet, pencil, and prizes
Procedure	1. Divide the students into groups of three. 2. Tell them that they have four minutes to find as many mistakes as possible on the application. 3. The groups tally up their findings. The group that finds the most errors wins a prize. 4. Point out that there were 23 errors on the application. Discuss the errors.
Time	15 minutes
Notes/Tips	Really emphasize the need for neatness, completeness, and accuracy when filling out an application.

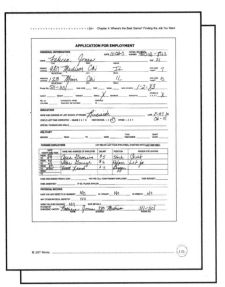

Activity: True or False: Completing Applications Takes Practice Students check their knowledge of how to complete an application.

Objectives	Know the various sections on an application
	Know what the wording on an application means
Materials	Worksheet and pencil
Procedure	1. Ask students to complete the worksheet on their own. 2. Go over the answers with the students.
Time	20 minutes

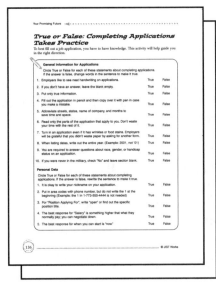

Homework: Practice Makes Perfect: Fill Out an Application Please Students complete an application that they can use as a guide when applying for a job.

Objectives	Gather the information needed for an application
	Apply knowledge of how to complete an application
Materials	Worksheet and pencil

Procedure	1. Ask students to complete the application in the workbook as carefully as if they were actually submitting it to an employer.
	2. Be available to answer questions students may have.
Notes/Tips	This activity can be done as a filler if you have extra time or as homework. Stress that it's important to complete the application accurately because they can use the information when they actually apply for a job.

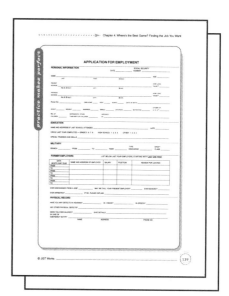

Activity: holla' zone Students write about attributes they have that would show a company they would be a good employee.

Objectives	Understand the importance of accountability
	Recognize how their performance reflects on other people
Materials	Worksheet and pencil
Time	10 minutes

Introduction Using the phone can be an important part of the job application process. It is important that students understand how to respond while they are on the phone with a potential employer.

Icebreaker 6: The Telephone Game Students play the telephone game.

Objective	Use proper communication methods when seeking employment
Materials	Script:
	I am looking for a job that will help me become more comfortable with people, gain management skills, and increase my employability after completing college. I am a responsible, hard-working, and loyal employee and aim to achieve beyond all standards that are set for me. I would make an excellent candidate for your staff and look forward to working with you soon. Thank you for your time and consideration.
Procedure	1. Students sit in a circle.
	2. Whisper the script in one student's ear and ask him or her to whisper it to the student to the right.
	3. Students continue passing the message on around the circle.
	4. Ask the last person to repeat the message.
Time	15 minutes
Notes/Tips	The point is that what is said on the phone is often miscommunicated or forgotten, so there are some important aspects of job phone-calling that must be remembered—which is the focus of the topic for the day.

(continues)

Session Six

Section Six

(continued)

Activity: Mock Interview Students perform mock phone calls about scheduling an interview.

Objectives	Understand the proper etiquette involved in talking on the phone
	Understand what to say when scheduling an interview
Materials	Two telephones and the following phone interview question guide:

> Instructor *(answering the phone)*: Good afternoon, *(inserting a company name)*. How may I help you?
>
> Instructor *(telling the student you are currently accepting applications and then adding the following [as best fits with the student's response])*: In order to apply for the job, you will need to come in, fill out an application, and meet with me for an interview. Before we set up an interview, though, let me ask you a few questions. What is your name?
>
> Instructor: Have you ever worked before?
>
> Instructor: What hours are you available to work?
>
> Instructor *(suggesting some times for interviewing)*: When would be most convenient for you to come in?
>
> Instructor *(giving the company address)*: Do you know how to get here?
>
> *End by telling the student where to go, whom to ask for, and what items to bring (for example: a resume, identification).*

Procedure	1. Ask an outgoing student to demonstrate how to respond to a phone call about scheduling an interview. (Do not provide the student with tips.)
	2. After the demonstration, use that conversation to point out good and bad aspects of phone calling.
	3. After the mock phone call, go over tips for scheduling an interview.
	4. Go into the role-playing activity.
Time	10 minutes
Notes/Tips	Be careful not to put the student volunteer down and make sure to stress that this is for learning and not an easy task. To volunteer is very courageous.

Activity: Role-Playing: Conduct Phone Interviews Groups of students use scripts of phone interviews to determine which person to hire.

Objective	Apply knowledge of phone etiquette to scripts
Materials	Worksheet and pencil
Procedure	1. Divide students into groups of four.
	2. The students read through the scripts on the worksheets.
	3. Ask each group to answer the questions.
	4. Discuss the answers.
Time	20 minutes

Homework: Answer Business Calls with Class Students evaluate their skills in answering business calls.

Objectives	Understand the principles of phone etiquette
	Apply the principles to personal situation
Materials	Worksheet and pencil
Procedure	1. Each student completes the worksheet, basing the answers on himself or herself.
	2. Discuss the students' answers, emphasizing beginning where they are and moving toward professionalism.
Notes/Tips	This activity can be completed in class if you have extra time or as homework.

Activity: holla' zone Students design a flyer to advertise their skills or for a job or position they want.

Objective	Use creativity in advertising
Materials	Worksheet or a separate poster board or piece of paper, markers, and other craft items
Time	10 minutes
Notes/Tips	This holla' zone transitions students into the next chapter.

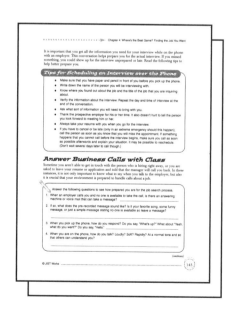

Posttest Hand out a short quiz to test the students' knowledge of the content after the presentation. (See the "Chapter 4 Test" section.)

Materials	Form and pencil
Time	10 minutes

Feedback Using the template in the back of this guide, create a feedback form that gives the students an opportunity to react emotionally and intellectually to the information presented in this chapter.

Suggestions and Teaching Tips

In Chapter 1, the students were asked to come up with jobs that they would enjoy working. When students first begin the job search process, it is highly unlikely that most will be able to actually work their "dream job," but when working on this section, remind students to look for jobs that will lead them on the path to their dream job. One example is to have a student look for work in a law office as a copier person, if they want to be an attorney.

It is important that they keep the bigger picture in mind while trying to find something that they can work at the present time.

Class Topics and Discussions

If you have a few free minutes or if you're having trouble engaging the students' attention or you know of particular situations in the lives of the students that could benefit from discussion, you may want to initiate a discussion of any or all of these topics:

- Ask students to talk with their older relatives about the differences between the skills that today's teens have and those required of teens in the past and then share their findings with the class.
- Talk about different experiences students have had in trying to get a job.
- Ask an employer to come in and share experiences or give tips in scheduling appointments for interviews over the phone.
- Bring in an answering machine and let the students practice recording messages that are acceptable for receiving business phone calls.

PowerPoint Slides

I have prepared several PowerPoint slides to accompany this chapter and present them here as pages that you can copy to hand out, convert to transparencies, or scan to create PowerPoint presentations. However, if you would like to have the actual PowerPoint slides, please contact your JIST representative at 1-800-648-5478 or check out our Web site at www.jist.com.

No act of kindness, no matter how small, is ever wasted.

Aesop

The Effectiveness of Traditional Job Search Methods

■ An average of 245 resumes are received for every interview granted.

■ Four of every five job openings aren't advertised.

Many times these unadvertised positions are filled faster than the advertised positions.

■ Many advertised positions are filled by people who never saw the job ads.

What Is Networking?

Two dictionary definitions:

- ◻ Network: any system of lines that cross; a group of people who work together informally to promote common goals.

- ◻ Networking: the promotion of political goals or the exchange of ideas and information among people who share interests or causes.

What Is Networking?

Networking is talking
to others to help advance
your cause.

Two-Foot Rule

Tell anyone and everyone within two feet of you what you need, and you will eventually find what you're looking for.

Outside Class Activities and Homework

What do you do if you know that your message isn't getting through to one of your students? Why don't you try a different approach? In this section, I offer a few suggestions that focus on the visual, auditory, and kinesthetic learning styles. Let my suggestions just be a starting point for you, though. Use your imagination, creativity, and knowledge of your students to come up with even more effective methods of communicating the message.

TOPICS	LEARNING STYLES		
	Visual	Auditory	Kinesthetic
Identifying skills	Students create a collage that Ilustrates skills teens have.	Write a rap that reminds kids that they have skills by listing some of the more common ones.	Play a version of Hot Potato in which students form a circle and students pass a ball to someone in the circle until the instructor says, "Stop" and names an activity, such as fixing a car. The person holding the ball has to name a skill developed in that activity.
Evaluating Applications	Analyze the applications collected and make a report on the similarities and differences.	Call businesses to find out whether applicants can pick up applications or must complete them onsite and compile a list to give to their classmates.	Collect as many different types of applications for employment as they can within an hour (or a time period you choose).
Creating a Phone Etiquette	Write a comedy of all the errors someone could make when receiving a phone call from a prospective employer.	Put together the sounds needed for the comedy.	Act out the comedy.

Chapter 4 Test

I always give a pretest as a way of introducing students to the upcoming topics and discovering what they already know. I do not discuss the answers on the pretest. I then administer the same test as a posttest, discussing the answers within the same class period.

Name _____

Date _____

Chapter 4 Employment Application

Read the following multiple-choice questions and circle the letter of the best answer.

1. What is the correct way to write "street" on an application?
   a. St.
   b. Street
   c. street
   d. Str.

2. What is the most effective way to find a job?
   a. responding to classified ads from the paper
   b. going out to businesses and filling out applications
   c. networking
   d. submitting your resume on-line

3. What are ways people can get work experience?
   a. volunteer
   b. internships
   c. work
   d. all of the above

4. What is networking?
   a. a sewing technique that uses nets to make quilts
   b. utilizing computer software to help you find a job
   c. a job search technique in which one asks others if they know of any job openings or ways they find a job
   d. a job search technique in which one submits his/her resume to employers at a job fair

5. What are ways people can find out more about a particular job?
   a. interview someone in that job
   b. job shadow
   c. read
   d. do an Internet search
   e. all of the above

6. What are two important things to remember when you are calling about a job?
   a. your name and the name of the person you are talking to
   b. where you heard about the position and the specific position you are calling about
   c. why you would make a good employee and when you can start working
   d. your school level and your past work experiences

Read the following true-false questions and circle the correct answer.

7. Applications should always be filled out in pencil.   True   False

8. You must answer questions that ask about your race/ethnicity on an application.   True   False

Use short answers to answer the following two questions.

9. List five different sources one can consult to find a job.
   a.   c.   e.
   b.   d.

10. What is the best response to "salary desired" on an application?

_____

Chapter 4 Employment Application Answers

1. b
2. c
3. d
4. c
5. e
6. b
7. False
8. False
9. Some responses: Networking, classified ads, Internet, yellow pages, go to stores, friends, family, school counselors, job training programs. Students may name specific Web sites as well.
10. Open or negotiable

Resources

Following are some Web sites and books that you may find helpful. Remember that Web site addresses frequently change. If a site is no longer active, try using a search engine to locate the organization that sponsored the inactive site.

Web Sites

www.jist.com–JIST Publishing, Inc., a career reference center

www.bestjobsusa.com–Best Jobs in the United States

www.careerbuilder.com–Online career service offered by a partnership between several newspaper companies

www.careeronestop.org–Publicly funded resource for people seeking jobs

www.careershop.com–Career Shop, services for people seeking jobs

www.computerjobs.com–Computer jobs

www.employmentguide.com–EmploymentGuide, a job search site

www.flipdog.com–FlipDog, a job search site

www.healthcareerweb.com–Health care jobs

www.hotjobs.com–The Yahoo! job search page

www.jobfind.com–JobFind, a job search site

www.monster.com–Monster, a job search site

www.monstertrak.com—The version of Monster for recent graduates

www.npo.net—Community service–related jobs

www.retailjobnet.com—Retail job site

www.students.gov—Government job site

www.youthrules.dol.gov/jobs.htm—U.S. Department of Labor work-related site for youth

Books

Edwards, Paul and Sarah. *Finding Your Perfect Work: The New Career Guide to Making a Living, Creating a Life.* (New York: J. P. Tarcher, 1996)

Ireland, Susan. *The Complete Idiot's Guide to Cool Jobs for Teens.* (Indianapolis, IN: Alpha Books, 2001)

Mattson, Ralph T., and Arthur F. Mills. *Finding a Job You Can Love.* (Nashua, NH: P & R Press, 1999)

Messina, Noreen E. *Teenwork: Four Teens Tell All: A Guide for Finding Jobs.* (Tinley Park, IL: Goodheart-Willcox Publisher, 2000)

Moore, Christopher Chamberlin. *What I Really Want to Do....How to Discover the Right Job.* (St. Louis, MO: Chalice Press, 1989)

Orndorff, Robert. *Peterson's The Insider's Guide to Finding the Perfect Job.* (Lawrenceville, NJ: Peterson's Guides, 2000)

Sinetar, Marsha. *Do What You Love, the Money Will Follow: Discovering Your Right Livelihood.* (New York: Dell Publishing, 1989)

Tullier, Michelle; Tim Haft; Marci Taub; and Meg Heenehan. *The Princeton Review: Job Smart.* (New York: Princeton Review, 1997)

Wilkes, Donald L.; Viola Hamilton-Wilkes; and Carl Carter. *Teen Guide: Job Search: 10 Easy Steps to Your Future.* (Alhambra, CA: JEM/Job Educational Material, 1991)

How's Your Game Plan Look on Paper?

Writing Resumes, Cover Letters, and Thank-You Notes

Chapter Objectives

- Understand the importance of a resume
- Create a personal resume
- Understand the role of the character reference sheet
- Create a character reference sheet
- Understand the purpose of cover letters
- Create a cover letter
- Understand the purpose of thank-you notes
- Create a thank-you note

Introduction

These sessions are designed to help students understand the importance of three career communication pieces–the resume, cover letter, and thank-you note.

Classroom Configurations

The classroom setup varies from session to session. I recommend that the desks are in a circle or semicircle rather than in rows. I generally try to start the classes with a whole-class activity or an activity involving small groups of two or three. Using activities gets the students involved in that day's topic in a hands-on way, engaging their attention right away.

Chapter Outline

Topic I.   Marketing Yourself: Building a Resume That Works

A.   Get Your Facts Straight

B.   Action Words Employers Look For on Resumes

C.   Learn from Examples

D.   Practice Makes Perfect: Resume for Work Experience

E.   Practice Makes Perfect: Resume for No Work Experience

F.   Check Your References

G.   Practice Makes Perfect: Reference-Building Worksheet

H.   What to Do with Your Finished Resume

Topic II.   Writing Cover Letters

A.   Cover Letters Allow You to Introduce Yourself

B.   Power Cover Letters

C.   Practice Makes Perfect: Create Your Own Cover Letter

D.   Your Cover Letter Checklist

Topic III.   Creating Thank-You Notes

A.   Thank-You Notes Make a Good Impression

B.   Practice Makes Perfect: Send Thank-You Notes

C.   Role-Playing: Choose the Best Candidate

Presentation Plan

The following section illustrates my methods of presenting the material to students, incorporating the activities found in the *Your Promising Future* workbook. You will want to adapt the methods and schedule to meet the needs of your students and situation.

Introduction When people want to sell something, they advertise it. Tell students to think of the job hunt as a way to advertise themselves. In order to do so, they need some sort of "marketing tool," a reason someone would want to hire them. In order to get the word out, though, they need to have something on paper. This is what a resume does: It is like a classified ad for one's self. This session helps students understand the function of a resume and formulate one that highlights their qualities.

Pretest Hand out a short quiz to test the students' knowledge of the content before the presentation. (See the "Chapter 5 Test" section.)

Icebreaker 1: Employee For Sale Use For Sale ads for houses or buildings (both descriptions and pictures) as a way of introducing self-marketing to the students.

Objective	Recognize the importance of careful wording to describe a product
Materials	Four or five For Sale ads with the text and the pictures separated, at least three copies of each of the ads, and prizes
Procedure	1. Divide students into three groups.
	2. Tell the students that they are in a race to see which group can correctly match the descriptions with the pictures.
	3. Distribute a set of For Sale ad descriptions and a set of pictures to each group.
	4. The winning group shares their answers.
	5. Distribute the prizes.
Time	10 minutes

Sessions One and Two

Notes/Tips   So what does looking at houses for sale have to do with writing a resume? Well, in ads, people choose words that make the houses sound beautiful, despite what they actually look like. The ads downplay or don't mention any negative aspects of the house, and they highlight all its benefits. Resumes do the same. They highlight experiences to make a person stand out and look good to employers.

Before going into the resume activity, it is very important to review the information in the workbook on resumes. Some students may have a difficult time coming up with items to write for their resume, especially if they have never worked before. If you have a class in which most have never worked, take some time to go over the No-Work Experience resume and brainstorm ideas with them. Also, take them back to Chapter 4, which talks about activities in which students have gained skills. The two sections, "Tap into Your Resources by Identifying Your Skills" and "Take Stock of What You Have to Offer an Employer," are the most helpful.

Activity: Practice Makes Perfect: Resume-Building Worksheets Students complete a template to create their own resumes.

Objective   Apply knowledge of resumes in creating a personal resume

Materials   Computer disk, computers, worksheet, and pencil

Procedure   1. Each student completes either the Work or the No-Work Experiences version of the resume worksheet.

2. Students type their resumes on the computer and save them to disks.

Time   35 to 60 minutes

Notes/Tips   The activity takes two sessions. In the first session, review the tips on resumes and present the two different formats students can choose from when writing their resumes: the No-Work Experience resume is for those with no formal work experience but can be used by anyone, or the traditional resume format is easiest if one has work experience. Have the students choose one of the formats and finish the worksheet before the next session. In the second session, the students type the resumes. Whatever the students do not finish in class they will need to do on their own before the next class. The resumes are due at the beginning of the next class.

(continues)

(continued)

(There is no set icebreaker for sessions in which students are typing resumes because they need as much time as possible to do the activity.)

I suggest that you have the resume templates on disk so that the students can easily fill in blanks. The resumes take longer to type without a template. Also, it is important to walk them through the steps of saving the resume on a disk if this is something the students haven't done in the past.

Homework: Practice Makes Perfect: Reference-Building Resume Students create personal reference sheets during the second session.

Objective	Understand how to create a reference sheet to use when applying for jobs
Materials	Computer disk, worksheet, and pencil
Procedure	1. Each student completes the references worksheet.
	2. Students type their references on the computer and save them to disks (as a separate file from the resume file).
Notes/Tips	This activity can be done either if you have extra time in the second session or completed as homework. These should be turned in and checked by the teacher.

Activity: holla' zone Students take an experience from the past and relate it to the shaping of their future, preparing students for writing cover letters and interviewing.

Objective	Analyze past experiences as skill-builders
Materials	Worksheet and pencil
Time	20 minutes
Notes/Tips	This holla' zone prepares students for cover letters and interviewing as it causes them to relate past experiences with their future goals. If they know how to articulate past experiences well, writing cover letters and interviewing will be easy for them.

Sessions Three and Four

Introduction This activity demonstrates the need for introductions and closings.

Icebreaker 3: Introductions Please Students try to complete a project without instructions.

Objectives	Recognize the importance of introductions
	Recognize the problems created by faulty communication
	Understand problems created by failures to work as a team
Materials	Lettered index cards, one copy of directions for each group
Procedure	

1. Students get into groups of three.

2. The groups choose a leader.

3. Tell the groups that each leader will get some directions and index cards. Stress that the leaders should read the directions immediately, but they are not allowed to show them to the other members of the group.

4. Hand the leader of each group the following directions, along with a group of index cards that have letters on them. The other students will not receive any instructions; they will just have to figure out what is going on.

   Directions: Do not explain to your partners what you are doing. Hand your partners some of the index cards you have been given and tell them to "hurry up and help me put them in order." You are to give no other instructions to your partners, even if they ask. This is your goal: Try to make the longest word possible out of the letters you have. When you have a word, don't say anything to your group. Just gather up the letters and bring them to the instructor and tell the instructor your word and how many letters it has. When you go back to your seat, don't say anything to the group. Just sit quietly until the instructor stops the class.

5. When all groups are finished (or after five minutes), discuss the activity as a class, using these questions:

   To the students who did not receive any directions: Ask them what they were supposed to be doing (what do they think the instructions were?).

   Did the leader help them try to figure out what they were supposed to be doing?

   Did they even figure out what was going on? How did they figure out what was going on?

   How did they feel when the leader got up and went to the instructor?

   Why did they think the leader went to the instructor?

   To the leaders: How did it feel doing this exercise?

   Did they feel like they were doing it alone or do they think their teammates understood?

   What would have made the project easier?

   What was the intent of the project?

6. Give a prize to the group with the longest word.

Time	15 minutes

(continues)

Sessions Three and Four

(continued)

Notes/Tips — Keep a list of each group leader, their word, and how many letters you gave them. The intent of the exercise is to show the students how difficult it is for people to understand why they are doing something if there is no explanation.

In addition, the students should begin to realize the necessity for thanking or closing an activity, that one cannot just walk away without saying anything and expect others to feel as though the project is finished. This activity is being tied to cover letters and thank-you notes because the purpose of each is to open and close the introduction of an applicant to an employer. If employers just receive a resume in the mail, they will probably just throw it away because they may not know what position it is for, they may think that it was left by mistake, and so on. A thank-you note after an interview lets the employer know that the applicant is still interested in the position and appreciated the time given to the interview. It leaves a positive impression on the employer and helps them to remember the applicant.

Before beginning the activities, review tips for cover letters and thank-you notes.

Activity: Practice Makes Perfect: Create Your Own Cover Letter Students write a cover letter for a mock position.

Objectives — Understand how to create a cover letter

Integrate list of skills with employers' needs

Materials — First session: Workbook, PowerPoint slide, paper, and pencil

Second session: Computers and disks

Procedure —
1. Review information about cover letters and thank-you notes.

2. Show the "Creating Your Own Cover Letter" PowerPoint slide.

3. Give the students time to write a cover letter with accurate personal information.

4. For the next session, the students type cover letters and save them on disks.

Time — 15 minutes for discussion, 15 minutes for writing the letter, and 25 minutes for typing

Notes/Tips   I have put cover letters and thank-you notes together for simplification and to show how the interviewing process runs along a continuum (rather than being segmented). Students should know that each piece ties into each other and the process is not complete until they have all been done.

These topics take two sessions. The first session focuses on learning about the two pieces, and students begin working on cover letters. In the second session, the students type cover letters and then complete the thank-you note activity. The addressing of the thank-you notes comes in the first session of the two just so the students can work at their own pace on typing. Those who are quick can move right on to the thank-you notes and not have to wait, and those who are slower do not have to stop in the middle of typing.

Activity: Practice Makes Perfect: Send Thank-You Notes
Students write a thank-you note.

Objective	Create a thank-you note
Materials	Worksheet and pencil
Procedure	1. Students work alone on this activity.
	2. The students think of something someone has done for them or a past interview they went to.
	3. Use the questions in the workbook in writing a thank-you note to that person.
Time	10 minutes

Introduction Students apply what they learned in the last two sessions and see how cover letters and thank-you notes function in a realistic setting.

Icebreaker 5: Recall Students are challenged to see how much they remember about cover letters and thank-you notes.

Objective	Recognize the importance of cover letters and thank-you notes
Materials	Pencil and two pieces of paper (per group), flip chart, marker, and prizes
Procedure	1. Break the students into groups of three.
	2. The students get out two sheets of paper and put their names on the top (or they can create a group name and write that on the top).
	3. Give the groups three minutes to come up with the purpose for each paragraph in a cover letter.
	4. The groups turn in responses.
	5. Give the students six more minutes to write, on the second sheet of paper, as many tips for writing cover letters and thank-you notes as they can think of (have them divide the two lists).

(continues)

Session Five

(continued)

6. While students are writing their tips, the instructor should be grading the first sheets to see which group has the most accurate responses.

7. Stop the groups and have them tally the number they have for each group.

8. Find out who has the most tips for each section and award prizes for each. Then go over the answers to the first section and let them know which group got them right (or the most correct) and award prizes.

9. Students call out responses for the second section and record them on the flip chart.

Time   15 minutes

Notes/Tips   Students must recognize the importance of these job-search tools and can gain much from a review of them.

Activity: Role-Playing: Choose the Best Candidate Students get to be the boss and make decisions on candidates based on their cover letter and thank-you note.

Objective   Recognize how cover letters and thank-you notes influence an interview

Materials   Worksheet and pencil

Procedure   1. Break students into groups of three or four.

2. The students read over the job posting and samples of cover letters and thank-you notes for that position.

3. Each group should decide which candidate would be the best for the job.

4. Ask the students to support their decisions.

5. Discuss as a class.

Time   25 minutes

Notes/Tips   There are no real right or wrong answers to this worksheet, but here are some best-fits:

Jose Sanchez would be my first pick because both letters were strong and he has extensive experience.

Marcy Raymonds would be my second choice because she wrote very strong letters as well. She ranks second because her experience is limited—she is just out of school.

Joe Josephs and Marc Jackson are a toss-up for third and fourth. Joe did not check the spelling on his letters, and Marc did not submit a thank-you note. Otherwise both would have made good candidates.

Stress to the students that the interview still plays a huge role in influencing the final decision, but these pieces are factors in that decision.

Activity: holla' zone Students find other uses for cover letters and thank-you notes.

Objective	To apply what they have learned about introductions and closings to other areas of life
Materials	Worksheet and pencil
Time	10 minutes

Posttest Hand out a short quiz to test the students' knowledge of the content after the presentation. (See the "Chapter 5 Test" section.)

Materials	Form and pencil
Time	10 minutes

Feedback Using the template in the back of this guide, create a feedback form that gives the students an opportunity to react emotionally and intellectually to the information presented in this chapter.

Materials	Form and pencil
Time	10 minutes

Suggestions and Teaching Tips

This chapter has very little group work because the students need to focus on putting together the resume, cover letter, and thank-you note. Make sure to spend adequate time on the resume and cover letters in particular. Review each student's work, and make suggestions for improvement. The goal is that the students save the resume, cover letter, and thank-you note and use them over and over again.

The area I found most difficult when working these sessions was the usage of the computers. Because I wasn't teaching a computer class, I did not have any influence on the students' knowledge of computers. I had to walk many of the students through, step by step, how to open up Word, open a file from a disk, begin typing, saving the file—really everything. It was a bit cumbersome and time-consuming, but extremely necessary in equipping the students for the future. The goal is self-empowerment; what you have to teach, you have to teach.

Class Topics and Discussions

If you have a few free minutes or if you're having trouble engaging the students' attention or you know of particular situations in the lives of the students that could benefit from discussion, you may want to initiate a discussion of any or all of these topics:

- What type of TV commercial makes you want to buy something? Do you prefer humor, beautiful colors, interesting background music, or a sense of reliability?
- How can you use networking to help you create a great list of references?
- Why is it important to thank people for their kindnesses?
- Aside from a job, what are other uses for a resume?

- What is the benefit of putting together your own resume and cover letter? (The greatest–you know and understand what you wrote and can easily articulate your experiences when interviewed.)
- What are some ways resumes and cover letters help you in the interview?
- What are some things you shouldn't put in/on your resumes, cover letters, and thank-you notes?

PowerPoint Slides

I have prepared several PowerPoint slides to accompany this chapter and present them here as pages that you can copy to hand out, convert to transparencies, or scan to create PowerPoint presentations. However, if you would like to have the actual PowerPoint slides, please contact your JIST representative at 1-800-648-5478 or check out our Web site at www.jist.com.

Resume Update

- *What is a resume?*
  A resume is a summary of your skills and experiences used as a marketing tool in the job search.

- *Who should have one?*
  Anyone who is eligible for employment.

- *How long should my resume be?*
  1–2 pages. An employer gives about 10 seconds of his or her time to reading a resume. So be concise yet powerful—you have only 10 seconds to catch his or her attention.

- *Why should I have a resume?*
  Employers want them.
  They organize your experiences efficiently.
  They help you recall past experiences.

Resume Do's & Don'ts

Do's

- ☐ Tailor resume to each job
- ☐ Spell-check and proofread
- ☐ Save to a disk
- ☐ Use clean, wrinkle-free paper
- ☐ Update often with new info
- ☐ Use accurate contact info

Don'ts

- ☐ Use **fancy** fonts
- ☐ Use bullets excessively
- ☐ Use words you don't understand
- ☐ Provide inaccurate employment date
- ☐ Send out with errors

What Is a Cover Letter?

- A brief, personalized letter that presents your resume

- Lets the employer know that you are interested in a specific position and demonstrates your ability to perform the job

- Provides brief examples of your qualifications

_____
Write your name

_____
Your address

_____
Your city, state, and ZIP code

_____
Your phone number

_____
Date

_____
Write the company name

_____
The address of the company

_____
City, state and ZIP code

Dear _____,

In response to your ad in _____, please consider my name for the _____ position. After reading my resume, I am sure you will agree that I will make an excellent candidate for the position.

I have varied experience in _____. I have spent _____ years in _____. I have also participated
           Skill or type of work   Type of work

in _____, which provided me excellent experience in _____ that would be beneficial to
   Activities related to position   Skill you gained

your company. In addition, you will find that I am _____, _____, and _____.
                                             Three positive characteristics

I would appreciate an opportunity to discuss my abilities in more depth and am available for an interview at your earliest convenience. I will be contacting you shortly so that we can set up a time to meet, but if you have any questions, please call (_____) _____.

Sincerely,

_____
Sign your name

Outside Class Activities and Homework

What do you do if you know that your message isn't getting through to one of your students? Why don't you try a different approach? In this section, I offer a few suggestions that focus on the visual, auditory, and kinesthetic learning styles. Let my suggestions just be a starting point for you, though. Use your imagination, creativity, and knowledge of your students to come up with even more effective methods of communicating the message.

TOPICS	LEARNING STYLES		
	Visual	**Auditory**	**Kinesthetic**
Marketing Yourself	Students write a classified ad, describing their skills to a prospective employer.	Students create a radio ad, describing themselves to a prospective employer.	Students create a collage, marketing themselves to a prospective employer.
Cover Letter	Students write a humorous script on how not to write a cover letter.	Students prepare a recording of their classmates' script.	Students act out the classmates' script.

Chapter 5 Test

I always give a pretest as a way of introducing students to the upcoming topics and discovering what they already know. I do not discuss the answers on the pretest. I then administer the same test as a posttest, discussing the answers within the same class period.

Name _____

Date _____

Chapter 5 Resumes

1. What is the function of a resume?

   _____

2. How long should a resume be?

   a. No more than 1 page

   b. 1–2 pages

   c. 2–3 pages

   d. length is not important, it should be as long as necessary to convey all your work experience

3. A cover letter

   a. tells an employer what skills you have.

   b. introduces your resume to the employer.

   c. is a letter written to your employer after you are hired to make sure you receive the pay you asked for.

   d. is attached to an application.

4. Why should you avoid using pre-formatted resumes and cover letters?

   a. They may have spelling mistakes.

   b. They are outdated.

   c. They don't show that you really are interested in the job.

   d. They are not addressed properly.

5. Sending thank-you notes after interviews

   a. is a way to show an employer your interest in the job and to thank him/her for their time.

   b. is only for people who kiss up to their bosses.

   c. is a technique that helps someone stand out to employers.

   d. a and c

Chapter 5 Resumes Answers

1. A 1- or 2-page summary of your life and employment history. It is designed to select specific parts of past experiences that will support your doing a particular job well.

2. b

3. b

4. c

5. d

Resources

Following are some Web sites and books that you may find helpful. Remember that Web site addresses frequently change. If a site is no longer active, try using a search engine to locate the organization that sponsored the inactive site.

Web Sites

www.jist.com–JIST Publishing, Inc., a career reference center

http://jobstar.org/tools/resume/index.cfm–JobStar Central, a job search site sponsored by libraries

http://resume.monster.com/–Resume page of Monster

http://www.10minuteresume.com/–Resume-building site that charges in one area but also has a free section

http://www.mgaa.com/kidscorner/resume.htm–An information page about resumes, sponsored by the Multicultural Golf Association of America, Inc.

http://www.yerc.ca/resumes.html–Resume page of the Youth Employment Resource Centre in Canada

Books

Farr, Michael. *The Quick Resume & Cover Letter Book: Write and Use an Effective Resume in Only One Day.* (Indianapolis, IN: JIST Publishing, 2000)

Farr, Michael; Gayle O. MacDonald; and Marie Pavlicko. *Young Person's Guide to Getting & Keeping a Good Job.* (Indianapolis, IN: JIST Publishing, 2000)

Nadler, Burton Jay. *The Everything Resume Book.* (Avon, MA: Adams Media Corporation, 2003)

Lathop, Richard. *Don't Use a Resume.* (Berkeley, CA: Ten Speed Press, 2000)

Resources for Cover Letters and Thank-You Notes

Check out these resources that will help you in writing cover letters and thank-you notes. Use these when completing assignments with the suggestions given earlier, and your cover letters and thank-you notes will impress anyone.

Web Sites

www.jist.com–JIST Publishing, Inc., a career reference center

http://www.aresumes.com/coverlet.htm–Arlene Schwartz's Personalized Cover Letter page with lots of free information

http://in.class.yahoo.com/careers/cl/mtcli.html–Cover letter information at Yahoo.com

http://www.jobinsight.net/cover_letter_samples.html–Cover letter page for JobInSight.net

http://www.soyouwanna.com/site/syws/coverletter/coverletter.html–Cover letter info on SoYouWanna.com

Books

Beatty, Richard H. *The Perfect Cover Letter.* (New York: John Wiley & Sons, 1996)

Kennedy, Joyce Lain. *Cover Letters For Dummies.* (Foster City, CA: IDG Books Worldwide, Inc., 2000)

Public Library Association and the Editors of VGM Career Books. *The Guide to Basic Cover Letter Writing.* (New York: McGraw-Hill, 2003)

Yate, Martin. *Cover Letters That Knock 'Em Dead.* (Avon, MA: Adams Media Corporation, 2002)

Ready for Tryouts?

Prepping for an Interview

Chapter Objectives

- Understand the role of a two-minute story
- Develop two-minute stories
- Develop techniques for handling tough interview questions
- Demonstrate ability to respond appropriately in an interview
- Recognize what is considered appropriate attire for an interview
- Understand how to make a good impression in an interview

Introduction

The interview portion of the job search is crucial, but often the most intimidating. It is the place where both sides–the interviewer and interviewee–come to find out about each other and how they can meet each other's needs. Many students, and adults, are nervous about interviewing, so it is important to work through the details of interviewing and help the students to feel at ease with the process. In this chapter, students will learn about questions that are commonly asked, behaviors that should be avoided, and questions to ask an employer, and they will practice interviewing.

Classroom Configurations

The classroom setup varies from session to session. I recommend that the desks are in a circle or semicircle rather than in rows. I generally try to start the classes with a whole-class activity or an activity involving small groups of two or three. Using activities gets the students involved in that day's topic in a hands-on way, engaging their attention right away.

Chapter Outline

Topic I.   Go in Prepped: What They'll Ask

      A. Tell Me About Yourself

          1. Think About the Future

          2. Remember Your Past

          3. Be Passionate

          4. Become One with the Company

      B. Practice Makes Perfect: Creating Your Own Two-Minute Story

      C. What Are Your Weaknesses?

1. Turn Negatives into Positives

2. Use Each Question as a Way to Talk About Your Strengths

3. Show Perseverance Through Tough Situations

4. Emphasize Educational Achievements If You Lack Job Experience

5. Be Respectful of Others

6. Don't Hide

D. What Are the Other Common Interview Questions?

E. Practice Makes Perfect: Answer the Interview Questions

F. What They Don't Need to Know: Questions You Don't Have to Answer

Topic II.   You Get to Ask Questions Too

A. Why Should I Accept This Job?

B. Practice Makes Perfect: Interview the Company

Topic III.   It's Your Turn to Shine: Acing the Interview

A. Dress the Part

B. Role-Playing: Choose the Professional Style

C. Watch the Time

D. What to Do During the Interview

1. Be on Your Best Behavior in the Interview

2. Close with a Thank-You

3. Don't Get Discouraged

Presentation Plan

The following section illustrates my methods of presenting the material to students, incorporating the activities found in the *Your Promising Future* workbook. You will want to adapt the methods and schedule to meet the needs of your students and situation.

Session One

Introduction The two-minute story is an important part of interviewing. It addresses one of the most common questions asked during an interview and can be used to help formulate responses to other interviewing questions.

Notes/Tips   Make sure that students have not done anything with the two-minute story exercises. Doing so will take away from the fun of the activity.

Pretest Hand out a short quiz to test the students' knowledge of the content before the presentation. (See the "Chapter 6 Test" section.)

Icebreaker 1: On the Spot Students are asked to answer this: Tell me about yourself.

Objectives   Understand what is involved in an interview

               Develop ability to think and respond appropriately in an interview

Materials   Script, pencil, and paper

Procedure
1. Read the instructions to the class.

2. Give students three minutes to respond to the statement, "Tell me about yourself."

3. Ask if anyone is willing to share his or her response with the class.

4. Discuss the students' responses and the level of comfort of the task.

Time   7 minutes

(continues)

(continued)

Notes/Tips   Here is the script to be read to the students before beginning the icebreaker:

> Think of a job you would love to have. Now imagine the company called you for an interview! You go to the interview, sit down, say "Hello," and the interviewer says to you, "So tell me a little about yourself." What do you say? You have three minutes to write your response. Ready, GO!

The following are issues that should be addressed in the discussion of this icebreaker:

> An interview is a way for you to learn about the company and the company to learn about you.

> It is NOT an outlet for you to beg for a job.

> The company is often just as desperate to find a worker as a worker is to find the job.

> The interviewee should come across as confident and capable.

> The interviewee should be prepared for the interview.

In writing a two-minute story, students should reflect on their strengths, weaknesses, and past experiences in both work and life.

Students can use their two-minute stories as a basis for answering many other interview questions.

Activity: Tell Me About Yourself Students think about their future goals, past activities, interests, and employability skills to help develop the two-minute story.

Objectives   Understand what information to add to the two-minute story

Recognize how to piece together various aspects of their lives and present them in a coherent manner

Materials   Worksheet and pencil

Procedure

1. Give students 15 minutes to fill out the four mini-worksheets in this activity on their own.

2. Students find a partner and discuss their responses together.

3. The partners critique the responses and try to think of additional responses to add.

4. Discuss the responses as class.

Time   30 minutes

Notes/Tips   Students can refer back to the resume activities in Chapter 5 to help in the "Remember Your Past" section.

The following are suggested questions to help the students in their critiques:

Does this response show that the person has initiative/is creative/will be a dedicated worker?

How does this activity relate to future goals?

Does this response reflect positively on the person or could it be eliminated?

What sort of employee does this person come across as?

If you were an employer, would you hire this person based on these responses? Why or why not?

Does this person come across as serious in his or her job search efforts?

What are some ways this person could improve the responses?

Practice Makes Perfect: Creating Your Own Two-Minute Story Students write their two-minute stories.

Objective	Apply knowledge about the two-minute story to create their own stories to use in actual interviews
Materials	Worksheet and pencil
Procedure	1. Students complete the worksheet.
	2. Students review what they have written and practice saying it. Encourage them to memorize it as best they can, but to avoid sounding mechanical.
	3. For next class, students should be prepared to answer the request, "Tell me about yourself."
Time	10 minutes
Notes/Tips	Have the students complete this activity at home to allow them plenty of time to think through the process and work on memorizing it. In the next session, the icebreaker asks them to give their two-minute story to a partner, but do not tell them this today. Just alert them to be prepared to tell their story.

Homework: holla' zone Students think of a past experience that has influenced their future goals.

Objective	Understand how past experiences impact future choices
Materials	Worksheet and pencil
Notes/Tips	You probably will want this worksheet to be completed as homework. Class discussion is optional, but it is important that each student receives feedback from the teacher.

Session Two

Introduction In the last session, you introduced one of the most common questions in an interview. In this session, you work on some more, often difficult questions to answer.

Notes/Tips   It is important for students to understand that in an interview they will have to be able to respond to all questions in a controlled and professional manner. No matter how difficult the questions may seem, they must remain calm and focused. The reason for going over some very tough questions is so that when it comes time for the real interview, students are prepared for anything and the interview will be a breeze.

Icebreaker 2: You've Got to Tell Somebody Students share their newly created two-minute stories with a partner–without the use of a script.

Objectives   Understand the importance of being comfortable in an interview-type setting

Demonstrate poise during an interview

Materials   Partners and two-minute stories

Procedure   1. Students choose a partner and then you number them as 1 and 2.

2. Tell the students that, starting with the Number 2 person, each will share his or her two-minute story without using notes.

3. Give the students three minutes and then tell them to switch if they haven't already.

4. The Number 1 person shares his or her two-minute story–again without notes.

5. Discuss these questions:

How comfortable were the students during the activity?

Did the students say exactly what they wrote, or did they forget everything?

What did the students learn from the activity?

Did they get nervous? If so, how did they react to the nervousness (forget, start laughing, fidget, and so on)?

Time   15 minutes

Activity: What Are Your Weaknesses? This worksheet is made up of six mini-worksheets that help students learn how to respond to questions that they may fear will make them look bad.

Objective   Demonstrate poise during difficult interview questions

Materials   Two flip charts, two markers, worksheet, and pencils

Procedure   1. Divide the class into two groups.

2. Each group writes down the questions on the flip chart and comes up with responses to the various questions within the worksheet.

3. One person in each group should record their answers on the flip chart.

4. Students should jot down some of the responses (that could be applicable to them) in their own workbooks.

5. After 15 minutes, have each group share their responses with the whole class.

Time	25 minutes
Notes/Tips	Students should take time to share some of their own personal stories in this activity, not just make up some answers that may sound good.
	You should oversee the groups and from time to time interject suggestions or hypothetical questions to help guide the students.

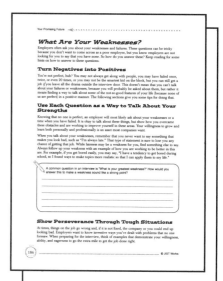

Homework: holla' zone Students write about a failure and what they learned from it.

Objective	Recognize the value of persistance
Materials	Worksheet, pencil, and time alone
Notes/Tips	You may want to use this holla' zone as a homework assignment. Class sharing of this activity is optional.
	Before students leave, ask them to come to the next class dressed professionally and read over the "Other Common Interview Questions" section.
	All the students will not remember to come dressed nicely. This is perfect. You will be doing a mock demonstration of a "good" and "bad" interview, so you want someone who is dressed for an interview and someone who is not dressed appropriately, but the students should not know this.

Introduction The best way to learn how to interview is to practice.

Notes/Tips	Before beginning the icebreaker, pull two to three students aside—two that are dressed professionally and one that is not. Explain to them that they will not be doing the icebreaker because they have a different task, which you will explain while the rest of the class is doing the icebreaker.

Icebreaker 3: Strengthen Me Students practice overcoming difficult interview questions.

Objectives	Demonstrate confidence during an interview
	React appropriately to difficult interview questions
Materials	The "Icebreaker: Strengthen Me" slide (in the PowerPoint slides section) and partner
Procedure	1. Students get into groups of two and select an "A" person and a "B" person.
	2. Display the slide or transparency titled "Icebreaker: Strengthen Me."
	3. The "A" person selects one of the questions to ask the "B" person.

Session Three

(continues)

Session Three

(continued)

4. Allow three minutes for responses.

5. The groups switch and the "B" person selects one question to ask the "A" person.

6. Allow three minutes for responses.

7. Briefly discuss the activity, using these questions:

    How comfortable were you doing this activity?

    What were some challenges to this?

    Do you have any other feedback?

8. Explain to class that two of their peers will be demonstrating interviews. For each interview, students should jot down some positive and negative aspects of each of the interviews. Discussion will be held after both interviews have been completed.

Time	10 minutes
Notes/Tips	While students are doing the icebreaker, assign the roles to the students who will be demonstrating interviews and explain what they will be doing. These students will then spend time preparing for the mock interview.

Activity: Mock Interview Two students demonstrate interviewing.

Objective	Recognize good and bad interviewing techniques
Materials	One desk, two chairs, two or three student volunteers, mock interview directions, and enough Interview Feedback Forms for the students to complete one for each interviewee
Procedure	1. Pass out Interview Feedback Forms to students and ask them to complete them during the interviews.
	2. Set up a desk and two chairs at the front of the room.
	3. The first interviewee waits outside the room, and the interviewer goes to the door and greets the interviewee.
	4. The interviewee and interviwer take their seats and begin the interview.
	5. At the end of the interview, the interviewer shakes hands with the interviewee, and they walk to the door.
	6. The interviewer greets the second interviewee and follows the same procedures.
	7. When interview is complete, ask all students to critique the interviewees.
Time	15 minutes

Notes/Tips | When students are critiquing, make sure they do not criticize the students who did the interviewing.

Acknowledge that this can be a very intimidating process so both should be commended for volunteering.

Even if the "good" interviewee made some mistakes, make sure that they were strong on eye contact, professional dress, professional speech, a firm handshake, appropriate body language and movements, and an interest in the position.

Activity: Practice Makes Perfect: Answer the Interview Questions Students practice interviewing.

Objective | Understand the process of interviewing

Materials | Workbook and pencil

Procedure | 1. Students get with a partner and select an "A" and a "B" person.

2. Ask students to turn to the "Practice Makes Perfect: Answer the Interview Questions" pages in the workbook.

3. Person "A" randomly selects four questions (one from each category) and uses the questions to interview person "B."

4. For each question asked, the students record the responses in the workbook.

5. Allow seven minutes for person "A" to finish interviewing.

6. Repeat the steps for person "B."

7. Students share whether they were comfortable during the interview process.

Time | 20 minutes

Notes/Tips | Another option is to ask people from the business community or other adults to come in and interview the students and provide feedback. This could also be done in a follow-up session to allow the students more opportunities for interviewing. In the Activities section, there is a form for critiquing the interviews.

Introduction This session is used as a review on interviewing questions. It should be used to address illegal questions in an interview and anything that came up while the students were practicing their interview. It should not cover elements such as dressing, behaviorisms, and timeliness, as those will be discussed later.

Icebreaker 4: Let's Get Shakin' Students practice their interview handshake and eye contact.

Objective	Understand interview etiquette
Materials	None
Procedure	1. Students go around the room, shake hands with classmates and introduce themselves (Hi, my name is…).
	2. Make sure that you (the instructor) shake their hands as well.
Time	5 minutes
Notes/Tips	This activity is to have the students practice their handshake and eye contact. At the end of this icebreaker, talk about the importance of a firm handshake and excellent eye contact during an interview. Some cultures frown on direct contact, but this is important when interviewing.
	This icebreaker was done to reinforce steps they should already know and make sure that students are comfortable with this process, as it is very important.
	This session will be a review of what they should know when it comes to the actual interview.

Activity: Interview Review Review interview information learned in this section.

Objectives	Recognize types of questions used in interviewing
	Identify the individuals' rights when being interviewed
Materials	Interviewing PowerPoint slides, flip charts, markers
Procedure	1. Students form groups of four.
	2. Review the PowerPoint slides about what to do if asked an illegal question and any other questions they may have remaining from interviewing.
	3. Groups come up with scenarios for overcoming obstacles (whether it be "illegal" interview questions or other difficult situations) during the interview.
	4. Students present their projects to the class.
Time	30 minutes
Notes/Tips	When putting together scenarios, encourage students to be creative. They can come up with a skit, write out a do's and don'ts chart, come up with some witty (yet professional) responses to illegal questions, etc.

Activity: holla' zone Students combat fears with positive thoughts.

Objective	Overcome pre-interview jitters
Materials	Worksheet and pencil
Time	10 minutes
Notes/Tips	Because interviewing can be difficult for some, be sure to provide some positive feedback, especially if students write about dealing with skeptical bosses or people who have been disrespectful because of their age or background.

Session Five

Introduction The purpose of an interview is not just so that an employer can find out about a potential new employee. What an interview is supposed to be is a conversation between the employer and prospective employee so that they can find out more about each other to see whether they are a good match. It's sort of like a dating game: The interviewer finds out about the candidate, and the candidate finds out about the company.

Notes/Tips	Finding out about the company helps to show interest and demonstrates maturity. When you are just looking for a job, you often don't care about what the company does or how you can benefit from your job; you just care that they hire you. But, when you are looking for a career, you pay more attention to what the job has to offer you and companies feel as though you will be a more long-term employee and an asset to the company.

Icebreaker 5: More About Them Students interview the instructor.

Objectives	Demonstrate interviewing etiquette
	Demonstrate a knowledge of interview questions
Materials	Paper and pencil
Procedure	1. Students break into three groups.
	2. Each group should come up with five questions to ask the teacher about the teacher's job.
	3. Groups then ask the instructor the questions they developed.
Time	15 minutes
Notes/Tips	Students should ask questions along the following lines:

Reason for going into profession

Benefits of profession

Type of schooling necessary

Opportunities available

Other career choices

Depending on your comfort level, you can advise the students to ask some more personal, professionally related questions, but that is to your own discretion.

(continues)

Session Five

(continued)

Activity: Why Should I Accept This Job? Students come up with questions to ask an employer to find out more about a company.

Objectives	Understand the need to learn more about the company
	Recognize acceptable questions to ask a prospective employer
Materials	Internet, worksheet, and pencil
Procedure	1. Students search the Internet for a job that sounds interesting to them.
	2. Ask the students to come up with ten questions to ask the employer about the company.
	3. If there is extra time in the class, students should investigate more about that company on-line. If there is no Web site for the company, they should try to learn more about that field and other companies similar to that company.
Time	10 minutes
Notes/Tips	Go over the "Practice Makes Perfect: Interview the Company" worksheet with the students. Make sure they are comfortable with interviewing a company. Another possibility if there is extra time in the classroom, students can pair up and practice the phone interview script for calling to interview an employer.

Homework: Practice Makes Perfect: Interview the Company Students call and interview an employer about the job available.

Objective	Demonstrate proficiency in asking questions of a prospective employer
Materials	Script, worksheet, questions, and pencil
Procedure	1. Students should review the script for calling a business.
	2. Students should call a business and set up a time to interview an employer.
	3. Interview the employer and fill out the worksheet with the responses given.
	4. Report on the interview.
Notes/Tips	When assigning this homework, make sure to give the students at least one week to complete it.

Activity: holla' zone Students write their impressions of the interview.

Objective	Evaluate their interview and relate it to their future interests
Materials	Worksheet, pencil, and notes from the interview
Time	10 minutes

Introduction Students learn how to dress for the interview.

Icebreaker 6: Fashion Sense Students put together a "fashion show" that presents what to wear on an interview.

Objective	Demonstrate appropriate dress for interviewing
Materials	Pencil, paper, markers, paint, newsprint, and fashion and career magazines
Procedure	1. Students get into three groups.
	2. Ask the students to come up with some sort of display to talk about clothing and the interview process.
	3. Hand out art materials, newsprint, and magazines and ask the students to come up with a way to talk about clothing for the interview.
	4. Allow 20 minutes for the project and then ask students to make presentations to class.
Time	30 minutes
Notes/Tips	Challenge students to be creative; if they want, they can come up with a skit or a fashion show, put together pictures of do's and don'ts, etc. Make sure that in their presentation it is brought out whether or not the styles they present are appropriate and why or why not. If they are doing something about "What not to wear," it is important that they demonstrate what to wear.

After students present their exhibits, have a discussion about dressing for the interview.

Activity: Role-Playing: Choose the Professional Style
Students look at photos to determine what is appropriate dress for a job interview.

Objective	Understand the importance of professional dress
Materials	Worksheet and pencil
Procedure	1. Go over what to wear and what not to wear.
	2. Students complete the role-playing activity in workbook. (They can work in groups with this if they would like.)

(continues)

Session Six

(continued)

3. In the worksheet, circle articles of clothing that shouldn't be worn during an interview.

4. Write down why these articles should not be worn.

5. Discuss acceptable attire as a class.

Time   15 minutes

Notes/Tips   When doing this activity, it is important that students understand why some types of clothing are not suitable for interviewing and what the alternatives are. If desired, when students are filling out the worksheet, rather than just writing out why the articles should not be worn, have them also provide a better alternative for that article.

Session Seven

Introduction In this session, focus on timeliness and the interview.

Icebreaker 7: On Time The students complete a puzzle in a given time.

Objective   Demonstrate how not being on time equates to not being complete

Materials   A timer and four 30-piece puzzles

Procedure   1. Divide the class into four groups.

2. Hand out a puzzle to each group.

3. Set the timer for two minutes, and have the students begin putting the puzzle together.

4. At the end of the time, stop students and ask how many have completed their puzzles.

5. For those who haven't completed the puzzle, ask what their puzzle looks like.

6. Engage in a discussion about how this can relate to being on time for an interview.

Time   10 minutes

Notes/Tips   When in discussion, ask the students to describe their puzzle, if it is not complete. Can they tell exactly what the picture is? Some may be able to make out what it is supposed to be, but point out that they still have to do some guessing and filling in the blanks. They would know more about that picture and it would look nicer if it were complete. This is the same way with being on time for an interview. If you are not there on time, your "picture" isn't complete, and you would look much better to an employer if you were complete.

Activity: Watch the Time Students read through scenarios relating to timeliness and interviewing and make the best decision for that situation.

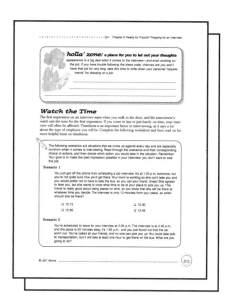

Objectives	Understand the importance of timeliness
	Understand the importance of effective communication before an interview
Materials	Worksheets and pencils
Procedure	1. Students remain in their groups from the icebreaker.
	2. Students fill out the worksheet as a group.
	3. Engage in class discussion.
	4. Review tips for timeliness.
Time	20 minutes

Homework: holla' zone Students write about how timeliness affects other areas of their lives.

Objective	Integrate the knowledge of the importance of timeliness with other areas of their lives
Materials	Worksheet and pencil
Notes/Tips	This can be done as homework or as a filler in the class. It would be beneficial to have a discussion about this in class, as being on time affects so many areas of their lives and is crucial to overall success.

Sessions Eight and Nine

Introduction This session should wrap up the interviewing section. The class will be going over how to act during an interview and how to close the interview.

Notes/Tips   This session should take up two class sessions. During the first class, the students will put together projects that will be presented in the following session.

Icebreaker 8: Be on Your Best Behavior in the Interview
Students evaluate common interviewing behaviors.

Objectives   Understand the impact behaviors have on prospective employers

Identify ways to improve behaviors

Materials   Worksheet and pencil

Procedure   1. Pair up students.

2. The students complete the worksheet in four minutes.

3. Students share their answers with the class.

Time   10 minutes

Notes/Tips   Review the tips in the workbook before beginning activity.

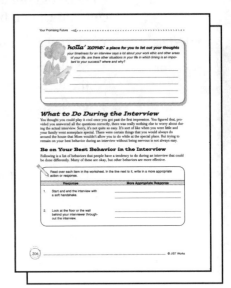

Sessions Ten and Eleven

Introduction This session will wrap up interviewing and answer questions students may have.

Notes/Tips   It is very important to encourage students to not give up when they begin looking for a job. So many students I have worked with, even at age 16, are discouraged about job prospects because of their color, their past, or their age. They need to understand that these obstacles, while frustrating, should not stop them. Yes, there are employers who won't hire them, but there are others who will. Everyone goes through rejection. The only way to overcome is to keep going. Eventually someone will notice their determination and give them the opportunity, but this can't happen if they quit trying, so they should never give up!

Icebreaker 10: Never Give Up Students share about a time when they didn't get what they wanted.

Objective   Understand the importance of looking at the positive side of disappointments

Materials   Paper and pencil

Procedure   1. Give students three minutes to write their responses to the following questions:

What is something you really wanted and worked hard for, but ended up not getting/reaching your goal?

How did you feel when you didn't get this thing?

Did you get anything from trying?

What did you learn from this experience?

2. Students partner up.

3. Give students two minutes each to tell their partners their story about the above questions.

4. After sharing their story, have the partners comment about something positive that could have been learned from the experience.

5. Discuss as a class.

Time   15 minutes

Notes/Tips   Often when we fail, we look at the negative side of the picture, but something positive always comes out of a trial, whether or not we choose to see it. This activity is designed to help students see that. Another quote to throw out there—it's not the end that matters, it's the means to that end that counts.

In relation to job interviewing, when people aren't hired, they may think that they did something wrong or were not good enough, but positive things to think about are

This gave me the opportunity to practice interviewing for a job that is better for me.

There were things about this job that I really was not interested in, so it's okay that I didn't get it.

There are more skills that I need to get before I can get this job, so this is showing me the areas I need to grow in.

This just isn't the job for me and there is something else out there.

Activity: Closeout Students put together plays or skits about closing the interview.

Objective   Demonstrate comfort with closing an interview

Materials   Pencil and paper

Procedure   1. The students get into groups of five.

2. Put the following phrase on the board: "Those are all the questions I have for you, so unless there is anything you have to ask, we are done."

3. Tell the students they have the rest of the class to put together some sort of skit about closing an interview. Each skit needs to start with the above line, but where it goes from there is on the students. Skits should be about seven minutes long.

4. Remind the students that at the next session students will perform their skits and questions will be answered about closing.

Time   30 minutes

(continues)

(continued)

Notes/Tips   If your sessions are more that 45 minutes long, this could all be done at the same time, but it is probably best to do this in two sessions to make sure all questions are addressed.

When students are putting together the skits, they can incorporate the following ideas in their skits:

> Questions about pay
>
> When the interviewee can expect to hear back
>
> Inappropriate questions to ask/comments to make at the end of an interview
>
> The interviewee hearing from the employer
>
> How to respond if you don't get the job
>
> How to respond if you do get the job

The students can also do more than one interview (i.e., a good and bad example).

When they are finished performing, have the students write any questions they may have about interviewing and pass them to the front. Go over the questions and answer them. You could also ask for students to answer the questions.

Activity: holla' zone Students write about ways they can stay positive during the job search process.

Objective   Create a plan for themselves to stay positive while searching for a job

Materials   Pencil and worksheet

Time   10 minutes

Posttest Hand out a short quiz to test the students' knowledge of the content after the presentation. (See the "Chapter 6 Test" section.)

Materials   Form and pencil

Time   10 minutes

Feedback Using the template in the back of this guide, create a feedback form that gives the students an opportunity to react emotionally and intellectually to the information presented in this chapter.

Materials   Form and pencil

Time   10 minutes

Suggestions and Teaching Tips

This chapter relies heavily on role-playing. This is to get the students comfortable with speaking in front of others in preparation for an interview. The various questions presented in this chapter all relate to questions that could be asked in an interview, so the students have plenty of opportunities to think about and prepare for the process. When they are done with this chapter, they should not have any hesitations about going to an interview, as they are fully equipped to answer almost any question that would come up. While going over this chapter, it is important to challenge students to come up with positive examples about themselves and to think of themselves as assets to a company. For many of the students I have worked with, this has been difficult, and it requires me as a teacher to really think outside the box and work with the students to come up with creative solutions for some of the obstacles they face.

Mock Interviews

You may want to have people from the business community come in to critique students' interviewing skills. Nothing will make the experience seem more real than confronting an adult who is going to ask questions. You will want to see that the interviewer completes an evaluation form for each "candidate."

List of Interview Questions

The following are a list of questions an employer might ask during an interview.

General questions

What can I do for you today?

What is the position you are applying for?

How did you learn of this position?

What kind of work interests you most?

What qualities are necessary to succeed in work?

What about this position interests you?

What can you do for the company?

Education

How much education do you have?

Do you plan on going to college?

What do you intend to study?

What are your favorite subjects?

What activities are you involved in at school?

Give me an example of a time you demonstrated leadership.

What is your least favorite subject?

Your grade point average is low. Can you explain why that is?

Work related

How would you be getting to work?

Do you have a driver's license?

What sort of work schedule were you looking for?

How many hours a week can you work?

Do you have any personal obligations that would hinder you from getting to work on time?

What shift would you want to work?

Can you work weekends?

Have you worked in the past?

What sort of experience do you have?

If you have never worked, what sort of skills do you have that would benefit the company?

What did you like most about your last job?

What did you like least about your last job?

What do you know about this job?

What do you know about our company?

Why do you want to work for this company?

Give me an example of how well you work with others.

How well do you take instruction?

What sort of management style suits you?

What are your expectations of a supervisor?

What do you do if you have a disagreement with another employee?

What would you do if you became bored with work?

Why do you think you would be successful in this position?

Do you work well under pressure?

You and your future

Describe your personality.

What is your major weakness?

What do you like to do in your spare time?

What is your most important accomplishment?

What are your plans for the future?

How does this position relate to your career goals?

What is your philosophy on life?

Interview Feedback Form

Use this form to rate the performance of this student's mock interview.

Position applying for _____

Name of Interviewee _____

Name of Interviewer _____

Quality	Needs Improvement	Adequate	Good	Exceptional
Firm handshake	❏	❏	❏	❏
Enthusiastic/ Interested	❏	❏	❏	❏
Friendly/Smile	❏	❏	❏	❏
Good eye contact	❏	❏	❏	❏
Speaks clearly, using correct English	❏	❏	❏	❏
Speaks honestly and openly	❏	❏	❏	❏
Gives concise answers/doesn't ramble	❏	❏	❏	❏
Seems knowledgeable about type of work	❏	❏	❏	❏
No obvious signs of nervousness	❏	❏	❏	❏

Comments

_____

_____

_____

Class Topics and Discussions

If you have a few free minutes or if you're having trouble engaging the students' attention or you know of particular situations in the lives of the students that could benefit from discussion, you may want to initiate a discussion of any or all of these topics:

● What do you do if someone has a really sad or bad two-minute story? How can you turn that into something good?

● If an employer asked you about your racial heritage, what would you do?

● How could someone who had been incarcerated for a crime present that in a positive manner during an interview?

● How can you judge whether your clothes are appropriate for an interview?

● How can you decide what you need from a job?

● What are some things you can learn from an interview that did not go well?

● Are there ways to "undo" a bad interview for a job you would really like to have? What are they?

PowerPoint Slides

I have prepared several PowerPoint slides to accompany this chapter and present them here as pages that you can copy to hand out, convert to transparencies, or scan to create PowerPoint presentations. However, if you would like to have the actual PowerPoint slides, please contact your JIST representative at 1-800-648-5478 or check out our Web site at www.jist.com.

Icebreaker: Strengthen Me

Choose from the following statements or questions:

- ❑ Tell me about one of your weaknesses.

- ❑ Tell me about a time when you failed.

- ❑ It appears that you don't have any job experience, so what sort of skills do you have to work a job?

- ❑ Have you ever worked with someone you didn't get along with? How did you work things out?

- ❑ What are some things you are willing to do to show that you are prepared to move past your past?

What Do You Do If You're Asked an "Illegal" Question?

- Don't act defensive. Inexperienced interviewers are just as uncomfortable in interviewing as you are, and they are looking for ways to ease into the interview.

- Answer truthfully if you feel your response will not hurt you.

- Inform the interviewer that the question is illegal. You may risk offending him or her and ending your chances for the position, but your integrity and knowledge may make you look more favorable for the position.

- If you choose to answer the question, base your answer on the requirements of the job and your ability to perform it.

- Be professional if someone asks you an illegal question and bring it to their attention. You can walk out if the questions continue.

What Do You Do If You're Asked an "Illegal" Question?

For more on labor laws and regulations, contact the Department of Labor at

866.487.2365 or www.dol.gov

For a federal Equal Opportunity Laws (color, religion, or sex) violation, contact the Equal Employment Opportunity Commission at

800.669.4000 or www.eeoc.gov

For a privacy issue violation, contact your own state's Department of Labor. To find out the number for your state, visit the Web site of the Department of Labor at www.dol.gov/dol/location.htm

Scope Out the Field

Questions to Ask When Trying to Learn More About a Company

- *Personal information:*

  □ Job responsibilities

  □ Describe a typical day

  □ Good and bad points about the job

  □ Challenges in the job

  □ The skills or personal qualities needed

  □ The potential for growth within company

  □ The potential for personal development on the job

- *Business related:*

  □ Products or services offered

  □ Length of time in business

  □ Work atmosphere

  □ Company mission

  □ Leading competitors—who are they and how do the two companies compare

- *General questions about the field:*

  □ What are the challenges in the field today?

  □ What is the future of the field?

  □ How has the field changed in the last ten years?

  □ Are any professional organizations associated with the field?

  □ How does an employee stay on top of new information for the field?

  □ What type of educational background do you need?

  □ Do you need any licenses?

Hip Alternatives
Interview Clothing for Guys

■ **No sports jacket?**
- Wear a rugby shirt, button down, or basic sweater.
- Stick to light colors, and only a few.
- DON'T wear clothes with the designer's name written on the front or all over the outfit.

■ **Pants dilemma?**
- Khakis and corduroys.
- Stop the sag; employers are not impressed by your boxers.

■ **Not into penny loafers?**
- Dress boots are okay if you are wearing khakis or cords, but not if you have on dress slacks.
- You can deal with some dress shoes if you have to...you need the job, right?

■ **Other fashion tips:**
- Wear a belt: It makes you look polished.
- If you have to wear jewelry, keep it to a minimum.
- If you have earrings, take them out, or at least wear no more than one.
- Keep the cologne to a minimum, if at all.
- No hats.

Hip Alternatives

Interview Clothing for Ladies

- **To top things off:**
  - Avoid tops that have words on the front, come off the shoulder, or have splits in the fabric.
  - Instead of a suit jacket, wear a solid-color, button-down sweater. You don't have to button it.
  - Don't wear tight-fitting clothes.

- **Let's get to the bottom of this:**
  - Avoid jean dresses or skirts.
  - Capri pants and shorts are not acceptable. If you wear pants, stick to dress slacks that are not tight fitting.

- **Other fashion tips:**
  - No hats.
  - Try to avoid fragrances, but, if you choose to wear some, keep it light.
  - Keep the jewelry to a bare minimum.

- **Most importantly, be as conservative as possible.**

Outside Class Activities and Homework

What do you do if you know that your message isn't getting through to one of your students? Why don't you try a different approach? In this section, I offer a few suggestions that focus on the visual, auditory, and kinesthetic learning styles. Let my suggestions just be a starting point for you, though. Use your imagination, creativity, and knowledge of your students to come up with even more effective methods of communicating the message.

TOPICS	LEARNING STYLES		
	Visual	**Auditory**	**Kinesthetic**
Two-Minute Story	Write out their story.	Record their two-minute story.	Play charades about their life. In this game, they can't speak and can only act out different aspects of themselves, and the class guesses what they're acting out.
Interview Etiquette	Write a script of an interview, illustrating what not to say.	Make a recording of background music and sounds to use with the script.	Act out the script about what not to say.
Interview appearance	Design a poster showing what not to wear to an interview.	Create a rap or song that tells what not to wear to an interview.	Prepare a fashion show that illustrates what is and is not acceptable to wear to an interview.

Chapter 6 Test

I always give a pretest as a way of introducing students to the upcoming topics and discovering what they already know. I do not discuss the answers on the pretest. I then administer the same test as a posttest, discussing the answers within the same class period.

After the pretest, you will find additional questions you may want to use, depending upon the requirements for the sessions that you're teaching.

Name _____

Date _____

Chapter 6 Interviewing

Read the following questions and circle the letter of the best answer.

1. The best candidate for a job shows up exactly when the interview is supposed to begin.   True   False

2. What is *not* a "two-minute story"?

   a. The story you make up when you are late for work and have no excuse

   b. A brief introduction of yourself that is used during an interview

   c. A concise response to the interview question "Tell me about yourself"

   d. A brief introduction of yourself that contains work- and non-work-related information that helps give an employer an overall description of you

3. When an employer asks about a weakness during an interview, the best approach to the question is

   a. Say you don't have any weaknesses

   b. Say that your weakness is work–you can never get enough of it

   c. State your weakness but show how you are working on it and that it won't interfere with your performance

   d. State that your biggest weakness is that you are lazy

4. Which of the following should *not* be demonstrated in an interview?

   a. Desire to work with that particular company

   b. Knowledge of most recent major developments in the industry

   c. Knowledge of what the company does

   d. Coming across as desperate for a job

5. If you have an interview scheduled but decide you are not interested in the job anymore, what is the best way to handle the situation?

   a. Go to the interview; you already set it up so you might as well check it out.

   b. Just don't show up. They don't know you and you don't want the job so it won't matter.

   c. Call the employer and make up some excuse as to why you can't make it to the interview. If he/she asks to reschedule, state that you have to check your schedule and you'll get back to them (but don't).

   d. Call the employer and let him/her know that you have decided you were not interested in the job so you will not need an interview. Thank him/her for considering you.

Chapter 6 Interviewing Answers

1. False
2. a
3. c
4. d
5. d

Resources

Following are just a few different resources to look into to help you with interviewing. You're sure to find all sorts of interesting information that can help you prepare for interviews.

Web Sites

www.jist.com–JIST Publishing, Inc., a career reference center

www.Careerbuilder.com–Online career service offered by a partnership between several newspaper companies

www.interviewcoach.com–Carole Martin's site on interviewing fitness

Books

Farr, Michael. *The Quick Interview & Salary Negotiation Book.* (Indianapolis, IN: JIST Publishing, 1995)

Eyre, Vivian. *Great Interview: Successful Strategies for Getting Hired.* (Independence, KY: Delmar Learning, 2000)

Kador, John. *201 Best Questions to Ask on Your Interview.* (New York: McGraw-Hill Trade, 2002). Available from JIST Publishing.

Kennedy, Joyce Lain. *Job Interviews For Dummies.* (Foster City, CA: IDG Books Worldwide, 2000)

Medley, H. Anthony. *Sweaty Palms: The Neglected Art of Being Interviewed.* (Berkeley, CA: Ten Speed Press, 2000)

Porot, Daniel, and Frances Bolles Haynes. *The 101 Toughest Interview Questions: And Answers That Win the Job!* (Berkeley, CA: Ten Speed Press, 2000)

Feedback Form

Name _____

Date _____

Please respond to the following questions as they relate to Chapter __. Your honesty in responding will help to improve this program. Thank you!

1. Before this chapter, were you aware of the information presented? If so, what did you know?

   _____

   _____

2. After going through this chapter, has the information you learned changed your attitude? Why/why not?

   _____

   _____

3. What are some of the specific facts shared that changed your mind?

   _____

   _____

4. How have these sessions changed your views about your future?

   _____

   _____

5. What are some questions that you still have about your future?

   _____

   _____

6. How useful were the worksheets?

   Very Useful   Somewhat Useful   Not At All Useful

7. Please comment on the worksheets.

   _____

   _____

8. What are some comments or suggestions you have for any of the sessions we have done in this chapter?_____

   _____

   _____

   _____

   _____

   _____

Workforce Development Skills

The following chart is a breakdown of which sessions correspond with the various workforce development skill sets.

CATEGORY	SKILL	SESSION(S)
Job Search	Employment Application	4-2, 4-3: Online and Newspaper Job Searches 4-4: Networking 4-5: Applications 4-6: Phone Skills
	Employment Interviewing	6-1: Tell Me About Yourself 6-2, 6-4 through 6-7: Other Questions and Etiquette 6-3: Mock Interviews
	Resumes	5-1, 5-2: Resume Builder
Computer Skills	Research	1-6: Volunteering 1-8: Career Exploration 2-5: Financial Aid 4-2, 4-3: Online and Newspaper Job Searches
	Writing	1-10: Career Search 5-1, 5-2: Resume Builder 5-4: Cover Letters
Career Counseling	Career Assessment	1-7: Career Inventory 1-10: Career Search
	Values Assessment	holla' zones 1-2: Defining Work 1-5: Personal Mission Statement 1-8, 1-9: Nontraditional Occupations

(continues)

(continued)

CATEGORY	SKILL	SESSION(S)
Vocational Exploration	Career Assessment	1-7: Career Inventory 1-10: Career Search 2-7: Interviewing Schools 6-5: Interviewing a Company
	Value Assessment	1-2: Defining Work 1-5: Personal Mission Statement 1-6: Volunteering 1-8, 1-9: Nontraditional Occupations
	College	2-1: Breaking Down Barriers to College 2-2: Introduction to Postsecondary Education 2-5: Financial Aid 2-6: Application and Testing Process
Work Habits (Please note: All sessions focus on strengthening work habits)	Life Skills	3-1, 3-2: Delayed Gratification 3-3, 3-4: Teamwork 3-5, 3-6: Goal Setting 3-7: Leadership 4-4: Networking
Leadership Development	Value Assessment	1-2: Defining Work 1-4: Overcoming Obstacles 1-5: Being Successful
	College	2-1: Breaking Down Barriers to College 2-7: Interviewing Schools
	Life Skills	3-3, 3-4: Teamwork 3-7: Leadership
	Employment Application	4-4: Networking
	Employment Interviewing	6-2, 6-4 through 6-7: Other Questions and Etiquette 6-3: Mock Interviews
Business Interaction	Value Assessment	1-2: Defining Work 1-5: Interviewing a Successful Person
	Employment Interviewing	6-3: Mock Interview 6-5: Interviewing a Company

Chapter 1 Additional Assessment Questions

Following are 22 questions you may want to use for assessment.

True or False

Circle True if the statement is true and False if it is not true, according to the information presented in this course.

1. You should always choose a job based on salary.   True   False
2. Everyone is capable of becoming successful and enjoying his or her job.   True   False
3. You can depend on finding someone to take care of you.   True   False
4. If you are not willing to live with the threat of failure, you will never grow.   True   False
5. People know inside of themselves which career to follow.   True   False

Multiple Choice

Select the letter of the best answer, according to the information presented in this course.

1. Most people enjoy their work more if they
   a. do the same task over and over.
   b. earn a good salary.
   c. work in a job that uses their interests and skills.
   d. realize that work is not something to be enjoyed.

2. What is the best way to select a career?
   a. Do what one of your parents does.
   b. Take whatever job you can find.
   c. Find a job in which you can do what you are good at and enjoy doing.
   d. Ask someone what would be a good job for you and stick with that.
   e. Do what your friends do.
   f. None of the above.

3. What is the definition of success?
   a. Having a lot of money.
   b. Being on TV.
   c. Achieving something you set out to do.
   d. Being popular.
   e. None of the above.

4. What is one way to become successful?
   a. Set goals for yourself.
   b. Just focus on making a lot of money.
   c. Try to get noticed by the media.
   d. Do whatever it takes, even if it's illegal.

5. Everyone who has become successful has had to
   a. cheat a little.
   b. struggle to overcome problems.

    c. fight against others who were trying to succeed.

    d. have connections with important people.

6. The two parts of a mission discussed in this course are

    a. convincing others to believe what you believe.

    b. making a positive difference in the world.

    c. using your talents and abilities in a way that makes you happy and helps to improve the lives of others.

    d. both a. and b.

    e. both b. and c.

7. How do you know if you are not truly fulfilling your mission?

    a. You are not making money.

    b. The way you are making a living violates or abuses other people's freedoms and rights.

    c. You are making lots of money.

    d. Your parents are not happy with your choice.

8. The purpose of volunteering is all of the following except to

    a. gain work experience.

    b. explore a career direction.

    c. get paid enough money to cover your expenses.

    d. learn about social issues.

9. Your personal success is determined by

    a. what others think of you.

    b. how you define it.

    c. the definition in the dictionary.

    d. none of the above.

10. One way to find what it is you are meant to do is to

    a. feel guilty.

    b. leave the people you love.

    c. take a career inventory.

    d. take an IQ test.

Short Answer

Write the correct answers in the blanks provided, basing your answers on the information presented in this program.

1. What are four things you can do to keep on track as you search for your mission?

    a. _____

    b. _____

    c. _____

    d. _____

2. What three places offer more information about careers?

    a. _____

    b. _____

    c. _____

3. What three areas should you think about as you choose your career?

    a. _____

    b. _____

    c. _____

4. What are two things a person must do in order to make dreams come true?

    a. _____

    b. _____

5. What are four fears people face when making changes?

    a. _____

    b. _____

    c. _____

    d. _____

Personal Opinion

Using your own personal opinion or experience, answer the following questions in the space provided. They have no right or wrong answers.

1. Do you agree with the definition of success presented in this program?

    Why or why not?

2. What is the best way for you to learn new information?

Chapter 1 Answers

True or False

1. False
2. True
3. False
4. True
5. False

Multiple Choice

1. c
2. c
3. c
4. a
5. b
6. e
7. b
8. c
9. b
10. c

Short Answer

1. Write things down. Start a notebook that you can use to record your career change process. Be patient. Be thorough. Spend time alone. Set aside at least 15 minutes a day to meditate and to think and write about your career/life investigation process. Identify your dreams and values—what is most important in life to you. Get involved. Find an organization where you can volunteer; that experience can help identify your likes and dislikes. Identify your fears. Involve your family. Have faith. Trust your instincts. Honor your dreams by not denying them on the grounds that they are impractical or unrealistic. Be open to change and new ideas. Never give up.

2. Libraries, bookstores, and the Internet

3. Interests, skills, and talents

4. Hard work and sacrifice

5. Not having enough money, failure, not fitting in, not having family support, not having good/any role models, not liking what you chose, facing ethnic/racial prejudices, overcoming poor grades/background, trying to reach a goal when you're already a parent, not being able to handle the responsibility, taking too long to reach your goal, being alone, and many more.

Personal Opinion answers will vary.

Chapter 2 Additional Assessment Questions

Following are 22 questions you may want to use for assessment.

True or False

Circle True if the statement is true and False if it is not true, according to the information presented in this course.

1. College is the only type of higher education that will get you a good job.	True	False
2. Most people face troubles on a daily basis, regardless of where they live.	True	False
3. One of the most important advantages of an education is that it opens minds to possible solutions.	True	False
4. A conservatory is a school that teaches skills such as carpentry and plumbing.	True	False
5. Often people need more education before they can improve their lives.	True	False

Multiple Choice

Select the letter of the best answer, according to the information presented in this course.

1. What type of school offers courses to students from the local area and is often used as a stepping stone to get into a university?
   a. Conservatory.
   b. Community college.
   c. Online college.
   d. International college.

2. What type of school offers training in shorthand, typing, bookkeeping, and other business subjects?
   a. Trade school.
   b. International college.
   c. Online college.
   d. Business college.

3. What are "free money" types of financial aid?
   a. Scholarships and grants.
   b. Scholarships, loans, and work study.
   c. Scholarships, grants, and work study.
   d. Scholarships, grants, and loans.

4. What is *not* a good reason for going to college?
   a. To make more money.
   b. To be able to help others.
   c. To feel proud of yourself.
   d. To know that you are better than people who don't go to college.

5. Scholarships are given for
   a. excellent grades.
   b. athletic ability.
   c. extracurricular activities.
   d. all of the above.

6. Although it may seem unfair, the people who get the most financial aid are those with

    a. the greatest need.

    b. the greatest knowledge about sources for financial aid.

    c. no interest in college.

    d. no intentions of applying for financial aid.

7. If you want to go to college, use all these sources for finding financial aid except

    a. the Internet.

    b. award search programs (that you have to pay for).

    c. school counselors.

    d. college financial aid offices.

8. When you're filling out an application for a scholarship,

    a. just be yourself.

    b. add extra activities to your list.

    c. get family members to write recommendations for you.

    d. call the office every day to see whether you got the scholarship.

9. You should really begin planning for college in the

    a. second semester of your senior year.

    b. second semester of your junior year.

    c. summer before your senior year.

    d. summer before your junior year.

10. Before you commit to a specific school, you need to

    a. find out whether the school will accept you.

    b. explore the campus.

    c. ask questions of students who attend the school.

    d. all of the above.

Short Answer

Write the correct answers in the blanks provided, basing your answers on the information presented in this program.

1. What are four areas you should consider when deciding which college to attend?

    a. _____

    b. _____

    c. _____

    d. _____

2. What are educational options for someone who doesn't want to go to college?

    a. _____

    b. _____

    c. _____

3. What two numbers determine how much financial aid a student gets?

    a. _____

    b. _____

4. What are some factors that determine the total cost of schooling?

    a. _____

    b. _____

    c. _____

    d. _____

5. What four numbers determine the total family contribution?

    a. _____

    b. _____

    c. _____

    d. _____

Personal Opinion

Using your own personal opinion or experience, answer the following questions in the space provided. They have no right or wrong answers.

1. Is it important for the United States federal government to make funds available for students who want to continue their schooling beyond high school?

2. Why is it important to know your options about higher education while you're a freshman or sophomore?

Chapter 2 Answers

True or False

1. False
2. True
3. True
4. False
5. True

Multiple Choice

1. b
2. d
3. a
4. d
5. d
6. b
7. b
8. a
9. d
10. d

Short Answer

1. Possible answers: Location, campus setting, school focus, type of school, competitiveness, cost, and so on
2. Trade school, business school, apprenticeships
3. Total cost of schooling, total family contribution
4. Tuition, room and board, books, personal expenses, transportation
5. Parents' income/assets and student's income/assets

Personal Opinion answers may vary.

Chapter 3 Additional Questions

Following are 22 questions you may want to use for assessment.

True or False

Circle True if the statement is true and False if it is not true, according to the information presented in this course.

1. When you get a degree from college, you don't need to worry about learning anything else. True False

2. Some core skills will help you in any profession and many other areas of life as well. True False

3. After a certain point in life, it's not your motivation and accomplishments– it's how you look that will get you to the top. True False

4. If you do not have the skills to complete an assigned project, you'd better find a different job. True False

5. The main reason for writing down your goals is so that you won't forget them. True False

Multiple Choice

Circle the letter of the best answer, according to the information presented in this course.

1. To reach your dreams, you must do everything except
   a. take any required steps.
   b. be willing to wait.
   c. earn enough money to buy them.
   d. ask for help, if necessary.

2. Delayed gratification is
   a. sending thank-you notes out too late.
   b. patience.
   c. patients.
   d. letting yourself have something as soon as you know you want it.

3. Some signs that people are not skillful in teamwork are all except
   a. taking all the credit for a group project.
   b. refusing to share.
   c. refusing to accept criticism.
   d. refusing to take all the credit for a group project.

4. Many companies are having "play days" for the employees so that
   a. they won't quit.
   b. they will feel more like a team.
   c. they will be healthier.
   d. they will be less effective.

5. Goal-setting is an activity designed to
   a. make a person better than everyone else.
   b. keep people busy.
   c. help people to improve their lives.
   d. drive students crazy.

6. When setting goals, remember to
   a. revise them daily.
   b. understand why no one else wants them.
   c. keep them a secret until you know you can reach them.
   d. share them with others.

7. A goal isn't good if
   a. it doesn't make you unhappy.
   b. it hurts others.
   c. it will take you a long time to reach it.
   d. someone else can reach it sooner than you can.

8. The good thing about leadership is
   a. it lets you break rules.
   b. you can use it to make a difference in people's lives.
   c. very few people do it.
   d. you can probably make more money if you're a leader.

9. Examples of leadership are all except
   a. you are the first one to get home from school.
   b. you are the captain of the team.
   c. you are a Big Brother or Sister to an elementary child.
   d. your boss asks you to train others.

10. Who will have to deal with the consequences of the problems in the world today?
    a. Your grandparents.
    b. Your parents.
    c. You.
    d. The people who report the problems.

Short Answer

Write the correct answers in the blanks provided, basing your answers on the information presented in this program.

1. What are some benefits of delayed gratification?
   a. _____
   b. _____
   c. _____
   d. _____

2. What three characteristics should every goal have?
   a. _____
   b. _____
   c. _____

3. Describe the difference between goals and wishes.
   a. Goals are _____
   b. Wishes are _____

4. What are four areas of life for which you should always have goals?

   a. _____

   b. _____

   c. _____

   d. _____

5. Leadership is the result of improving what three qualities?

   a. _____

   b. _____

   c. _____

Personal Opinion

Relying on your own personal opinion or experience, answer the following questions in the space provided.

1. Who, in your life, has demonstrated the most patience that led to achieving goals?

2. When someone mentions the word leader, who comes to your mind and why?

Chapter 3 Answers

True or False

1. False
2. True
3. False
4. False
5. True

Multiple Choice

1. c
2. b
3. d
4. b
5. c
6. d
7. b
8. b
9. a
10. c

Short Answer

1. Possible answers: More prepared, can appreciate what you get, better opportunities open up, a brighter future

2. Attainable, measurable, time limit

3. Goals are desires that have action plans attached to them.

   Wishes are things that people want but do not do anything to make that want a reality.

4. Mental, physical, family, spiritual, financial, social, and career

5. Patience, teamwork, and goal setting

Personal Opinion answers will vary.

Chapter 4 Additional Assessment Questions

Following are 22 questions you may want to use for assessment.

True or False

Circle True if the statement is true and False if it is not true, according to the information presented in this course.

1.	Taking care of brothers and sisters requires skills that can be useful in getting and keeping a job.	True	False
2.	If you don't have all the skills mentioned in a classified ad, just lie. You can probably learn everything you need to know quickly, and no one will be the wiser.	True	False
3.	The government has established laws to protect the young from unethical employers.	True	False
4.	The quickest way to get a job is through the Internet.	True	False
5.	You should just be yourself on the phone. If an employer can't accept you the way you are, that's his or her problem.	True	False

Multiple Choice

Select the letter of the best answer, according to the information presented in this course.

1. Where do we gain skills we can use in our jobs? Choose the best answer from the following choices.

   a. School.

   b. Church.

   c. Home.

   d. All of the above.

2. According to this chapter, what is a transferable skill?

   a. Those you can use in any job.

   b. Those you can teach to others.

   c. Those someone taught to you.

   d. None of the above.

3. What is a personal skill?

   a. One that benefits only yourself.

   b. One that reflects your personality.

   c. One that an employer teaches you on a one-on-one basis.

   d. All of the above.

4. What do you need in order to successfully use classified ads or the Internet to get a job?

   a. A computer.

   b. A TV.

   c. A newspaper subscription.

   d. A good idea of what you want and your skills.

5. What does the author mean when she refers to networking?

   a. Using the Internet to get a job.

   b. Connecting your computer to another computer.

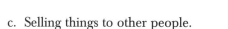

    c. Selling things to other people.

    d. Talking to people in order to get something you may need or want.

6. Whose names should you definitely not use as references?

    a. Family members.

    b. Best friends.

    c. Former employers.

    d. Teachers.

7. When you're filling out an application, complete

    a. only the questions that apply to you.

    b. only the questions that you understand.

    c. only the questions that you can answer truthfully.

    d. everything that is not marked "Do Not Write in This Area. For Office Use Only."

8. When is usually the best time to make a good impression when you're seeking a job?

    a. During the interview.

    b. During your talk with the recruiter or employer on the phone.

    c. Your first day on the job.

    d. During the training session.

9. What should you do if you feel nervous about talking on the phone?

    a. Ask your friend to call and pretend to be you.

    b. Focus on the fact that the employer wants to make you look bad to find out what you're made of.

    c. Realize that the employer is desperately looking for someone who can fill the position.

    d. Never use the phone. Always apply in person.

10. In addition to knowing what to say when an employer calls, what else is important?

    a. That you know how much money you need to earn in order to accept the job.

    b. That your environment is prepared to handle the call.

    c. That you know the person's name.

    d. That you be at home when the employer calls.

Short Answer

Write the correct answers in the blanks provided, basing your answers on the information presented in this program.

1. What should you do if you don't have all the skills the employer requests?

    a. _____

    b. _____

2. Why do many people end up disliking a job that they accepted?

    a. _____

    b. _____

    c. _____

3. What do you need to know in order to be able to network?

    a. _____

    b. _____

    c. _____

4. What is the difference between part-time and seasonal hours? (Complete each statement.)

    a. Part-time is _____

    b. Seasonal is _____

5. What often happens if an employer is treated disrespectfully on the phone, even if it was unintentional? _____

Personal Opinion

Using on your own personal opinion or experience, answer the following questions in the space provided. They have no right or wrong answers.

1. How important is networking in your life?

2. Is it more important to be yourself or act like a professional when you're trying to get a job?

Chapter 4 Answers

True or False
1. True
2. False
3. True
4. False
5. False

Multiple Choice
1. d
2. a
3. b
4. d
5. d
6. a
7. d
8. b
9. c
10. b

Short Answer

1. Compare all the skills you have with those the job requires. Emphasize the skills that the job requires. To make up for skills you don't have, show how your skills that were not requested can make you an asset to the company. If you present all your skills well, you can still get the job even if you lack some of the qualifications.

2. They didn't do their homework, find several employers to pick from, and look for an employer who best matches their needs and skills.

3. To be able to network, you need to know what you want, how you tap into resources that will help you get there, and how to make yourself valuable.

4. a. Part-time is working less than 35 hours a week.

    b. Seasonal is working (either full- or part-time) for a company for a short period of time (such as during the summer or holidays).

5. The person looking for a job is not asked to interview.

Personal Opinion answers will vary.

Chapter 5 Additional Assessment Questions

Following are 22 questions you may want to use for assessment.

True or False

Circle True if the statement is true and False if it is not true, according to the information presented in this course.

1. Employers rarely ask teens for resumes.	True	False
2. The longer your resume, the more it will impress the employer.	True	False
3. The purpose of a cover letter is to give the employer a reason to read your resume.	True	False
4. Faxing is the most common way of getting a resume to a company.	True	False
5. Do not be too concerned about grammar when you're writing a thank-you note. Getting it there quickly is what is important.	True	False

Multiple Choice

Select the letter of the best answer, according to the information presented in this course.

1. What is the best way to be noticed by an employer?

    a. Put together a video about yourself.

    b. Walk into his/her office without an appointment.

    c. Send a resume.

    d. Submit an application.

2. Where do you come up with the information to write on a resume?

    a. From a book about resumes.

    b. Copy the requirements the job description asks for.

    c. Make it up.

    d. Select experiences from your past.

3. The length of time an employer spends reading a resume is

    a. 10 seconds.

    b. 2 minutes.

    c. 30 seconds.

    d. 1 minute.

4. The most effective resumes

    a. are handwritten.

    b. have fancy fonts and pictures on them.

    c. are written for a specific job and refer to the requirements of the position.

    d. are short.

5. When providing references, make sure

    a. it is someone you have known at least a month.

    b. you submit the sheet with your resume.

    c. you ask people if you can use their names as references.

    d. you provide an evening phone number.

6. The second paragraph in a cover letter should
   a. state how you learned about the position.
   b. highlight your experiences that relate to the job.
   c. ask to schedule a time to interview.
   d. include your resume.

7. "I would welcome the opportunity for a personal interview to further discuss my qualifications" is an example of
   a. a powerful close.
   b. a powerful introduction.
   c. someone who is trying to kiss up to an employer.
   d. a powerful cover letter.

8. What is the best way to submit any business communication?
   a. By mail.
   b. Typed.
   c. Handwritten.
   d. Wrinkled.

9. Which of the following is not true for both cover letters and thank-you notes?
   a. They should be direct and to the point.
   b. They should not demonstrate enthusiasm for the job.
   c. They should be typed.
   d. They should be signed by you.

10. How soon should you send a thank-you note to an employer?
    a. Within a week.
    b. Within 38 hours.
    c. Within 24 hours.
    d. Within 48 hours.

Short Answer

Write the correct answers in the blanks provided, basing your answers on the information presented in this program.

1. What sections should a resume include?
   a. _____
   b. _____
   c. _____
   d. _____

2. What types of paragraphs should a cover letter include?
   a. _____
   b. _____
   c. _____

3. Whose names should you NOT use on a reference sheet?
   a. _____
   b. _____

4. What information should you provide for each reference?

   a. _____

   b. _____

   c. _____

   d. _____

5. What is the most important point a thank-you note demonstrates? _____

Personal Opinion

Using your own personal opinion or experience, answer the following questions in the space provided. They have no right or wrong answers.

1. What does creating a resume show you about yourself?

2. How important are the names you list on a reference sheet?

Chapter 5 Answers

True or False

1. True
2. False
3. True
4. True
5. False

Multiple Choice

1. c
2. d
3. a
4. c
5. c
6. b
7. a
8. b
9. c
10. d

Short Answer

1. Personal contact information, Education, Work history, Skills

2. Introduction, Body, Close

3. Possible answers: Family members and people you've know less than a year, someone who will not say good things about you

4. Name, how you know them, place of employment, job title, daytime phone number

5. That you are the best person for the job

Personal Opinion answers will vary.

Chapter 6 Additional Assessment Questions

Following are 22 questions you may want to use for assessment.

True or False

Circle True if the statement is true and False if it is not true, according to the information presented in this course.

1. Most employers really want to hire the person they're interviewing.		True	False
2. If you get the interview, you can count on getting hired.		True	False
3. Employers want to see who you truly are so wear your everyday clothes.		True	False
4. Do your best to get to an interview on time because being late makes a bad impression on the employer.		True	False
5. If a company turns you down for a job, you can sue them.		True	False

Multiple Choice

Select the letter of the best answer, according to the information presented in this course.

1. As far as you're concerned, the two purposes of interviewing for a job are
    a. self-marketing and learning more about the company to see whether you want to work there.
    b. gaining experience in public speaking and finding out about careers.
    c. learning poise and learning self-confidence.
    d. letting the employer decide whether they like you and how much they'll pay you.

2. The crucial part of a job search is the
    a. application.
    b. cover letter.
    c. scheduling of the appointment.
    d. interview.

3. A two-minute story does not include your
    a. family history.
    b. strengths.
    c. interests.
    d. experiences.

4. When is the best time to give an employer the sense that you have passion for the job?
    a. When you're scheduling the interview.
    b. Before the interview begins.
    c. During the interview.
    d. Never, because you don't want to look needy.

5. If an employer asks you what your weaknesses are, you should
    a. plead the Fifth Amendment.
    b. politely refuse to answer because employers are not allowed to ask questions like that.
    c. talk about what you've learned and how you've grown because of the negative things in your life.
    d. apologize for all the bad things you've done and promise never to do them again.

6. Employers will ask you how you would handle a negative situation on the job because
    a. they want to know if you can suggest inventive ways to deal with problems that no one fore-saw.
    b. they want to see whether you're honest.
    c. they are trying to get suggestions for problems they haven't been able to solve.
    d. they aren't prepared to interview you.

7. If you have no work experience, you should
    a. lie and say that you do. Most employers never check your records anyway.
    b. provide examples of how you can use skills required at school on the job.
    c. give up. The company won't hire you anyway.
    d. really emphasize how much your family and you need for you to be working.

8. If an employer asks you an illegal question, you should NOT

    a. make a big scene.

    b. bring it to the employer's attention.

    c. politely refuse to answer.

    d. answer truthfully if you feel your response will not hurt you.

9. To get a job, you must make sure that your clothes

    a. are expensive.

    b. are the latest fad so that the employers are impressed.

    c. are acceptable for the business place where you're interviewing.

    d. don't make you look too nerdy.

10. At the end of the interview, you should

    a. ask how much the pay is and when you can start.

    b. thank the interviewer.

    c. close the door.

    d. hang around and talk to the employees so that you know what the job is like.

Short Answer

Write the correct answers in the blanks provided, basing your answers on the information presented in this program.

1. Rather than think, "I really need a job, please let them hire me," think of the employer as saying _____

2. List three topics employers cannot ask you about.

    a. _____

    b. _____

    c. _____

3. Write four questions you should ask the employer.

    a. _____

    b. _____

    c. _____

    d. _____

4. The focus of the interview is on what?

    _____

5. List three reasons why you should get to the interview a few minutes early.

    a. _____

    b. _____

    c. _____

Personal Opinion

Using on your own personal opinion or experience, answer the following questions in the space provided. They have no right or wrong answers.

1. Why is it important for you to prepare for an interview?

2. Should you try to act and talk professionally on the job, or should you just be yourself?

Chapter 6 Answers

True or False

1. True
2. False
3. False
4. True
5. False

Multiple Choice

1. a
2. d
3. a
4. c
5. c
6. a
7. b
8. a
9. c
10. b

Short Answer

1. "We really need a quality employee. Could this be that person?" It's as though they are saying, "*Please* let this be the right person. We're tired of interviewing, and we really need someone."

2. Possible answers:
   Gender, religion, marital status, age, physical and/or mental status, ethnic background, country of origin, sexual preference, any other discriminatory factors that are illegal for making employment decisions

3. Possible answers:

   Job responsibilities

   Describe a typical day

   Good and bad points about the job

   Challenges in the job

   The skills or personal qualities needed

   The potential for growth within the company

   The potential for personal development on the job

   The products or services offered

   Length of time in business

   Work atmosphere

   Company mission

   Leading competitors—who are they and how do the two companies compare?

   What are the challenges in the field today?

   What is the future of the field?

   How has the field changed in the last ten years?

   Are any professional organizations associated with the field?

   How does an employee stay on top of new information for the field?

   What type of educational background do you need?

   Do you need any licenses?

4. The interview needs to be focused on you and your skills, not how you look and smell.

5. Arriving early to an interview not only looks good to an employer, but also will allow you some extra time to prepare. Here are some other benefits:

   - Gives you time to collect yourself and relax before the interview

   - Provides time to investigate and find out more about the company, as you will often find literature and other information about the company in the waiting area

   - Allows you to fix your hair, clothes, makeup, or anything else that may be out of place from the commute

   - Lets you check out the work environment to see whether it's a place you would feel comfortable working in

Personal Opinion answers may vary.